IN DEFENSE OF POLITICAL PHILOSOPHY—

A Reply to Robert Paul Wolff's
In Defense of Anarchism

*the text of this book is printed
on 100% recycled paper*

Jeffrey H. Reiman

IN DEFENSE
OF POLITICAL
PHILOSOPHY

A Reply to Robert Paul Wolff's
In Defense of Anarchism

HARPER TORCHBOOKS ❧
HARPER & ROW, PUBLISHERS
NEW YORK · EVANSTON · SAN FRANCISCO · LONDON

IN DEFENSE OF POLITICAL PHILOSOPHY—A REPLY TO ROBERT PAUL
WOLFF'S *In Defense of Anarchism*

First HARPER TORCHBOOK edition published 1972

LIBRARY OF CONGRESS CATALOG CARD NUMBER: 72-80550

STANDARD BOOK NUMBER: 06-131684-9

Designed by Yvette A. Vogel

for Rosalind

Acknowledgments

The world of ideas is a shared world, and whoever undertakes to put some ideas into the form of a book acts as a funnel through which thoughts and arguments, developed in interactions with others, take on a particular form at a particular time. The present work is no exception, and the present acknowledgments can only reflect a fraction of the debt owed to teachers and colleagues. I am particularly grateful to Professors David Sprintzen of the Department of Philosophy at C. W. Post and John Wildeman of the Department of Sociology at Hofstra University for reading earlier versions of the manuscript and making valuable comments and recommendations. A word of thanks must also be given to Gail Tarleton for diligently and carefully typing the various drafts of the present manuscript, from first to final.

A first book is perhaps not an inappropriate occasion to acknowledge—though not to settle—a first intellectual debt to the teacher and philosopher who first introduced me to the excitement and urgency of the philosophical life, Professor John J. McDermott of the Department of Philosophy at Queens College in the City University of New York.

Finally, my wife has read and re-read all the drafts of the manuscript, making important suggestions on style and content, so that if the present book is at all readable, she deserves some of the credit. And precisely because this is really the least important way in which she has contributed to the present work, this book is dedicated to her.

J. H. R.

Contents

Bereft of political solutions to political problems,
idealizing individualistic rebellion, anarchism reflects
the extent of our difficulties rather than effects
significant alteration of them, but the will to criticize
the excesses of organization is the positive note of
fresh air when the breathing of these organisms
becomes labored and stifling.

> *Irving L. Horowitz,*
> *"A Postscript to 'The Anarchists' "*

In sum, the ultimate animus of anarchism is a deep
sense of the crime which an enforced organization
inflicts upon life, which is by birthright free,
individual, varied.

> *William Ernest Hocking,*
> *"Anarchism and Consent"*

In the present century, the state has grown so great
that opposition to its authority seems merely quixotic;
the crimes committed in the name of the state,
unfortunately, have also been so great that we cannot
shun the obligation to examine the grounds of its
authority and subject them to rigorous critique.

> *Robert Paul Wolff,*
> Political Man and Social Man

Preface

To the philosopher painting in broad strokes, the changes in the American political imagination during the last decade must appear particularly fateful. The late sixties seem to have ushered in a skepticism about American institutions without historical precedent. Many things have contributed to this, not the least of which is the pervasiveness of mass media and the existence of a generation for which affluence was not a reward for sacrifices bravely borne but a fact of life. Young whites for whom the American dream was never merely a dream and young blacks for whom it was always merely a dream could not help but sense the reality of America differently than that generation which had nurtured the dream in depression here or poverty abroad, and saw it become reality in the prosperity which followed the second world war.

The politics of a nation is one thing; its political imagination is quite another. Politics amounts to the day-to-day decisions and actions of politicians and their audiences. But political imagination refers to that sense of the connection between the real and the ideal, and the boundary between the possible and the utopian, which is felt before it is reasoned out. It is one of the abiding tasks of political philosophy to clarify the political imagination of a people, to think it through consistently, to link it up to the accumulated insights of past generations and to sound its resources for supplying guidance for choices yet to be made. It has been the continuing effect of political philosophy, if not always the intent of political philosophers, to forge the inchoate political imagination of a people, of a generation, of a class, of a sect, of a nation into an image of the world as it should and could be and a demand for the action to make it so. Hence the conflicts and convergences which have recently characterized the American political imagination ought to be carefully attended to, since they may provide a fertile source for a new vision of social and political reality.

Those Americans for whom affluence has been the realization of *their* dream possess a political imagination which sensed little tension between the realities and ideals of American institutions, between the possible and the utopian. Those, on the other hand, for whom affluence or oppressive poverty were simple facts of life felt a painful distance between the real and the ideal. They felt their possibilities constrained to narrow paths and their utopias impossible.

On the level of political imagination—if not on the level of politics—the short-lived presidency of John Kennedy may have offered the last attempt to heal this breach. Reason and innovation seemed to be at the helm of American institutions, and the dissonances between the real and the ideal could be no more than temporary. In time youth would defeat age, intelligence would defeat poverty and youthful idealism could be seen any weekend playing touch football on the White House lawn.

But Kennedy was killed, and his successors made no bones about the fact that the business of politics is power. The obviousness of the immorality of the Asian war grew and with it the brazenness of the duplicity in its defense. And all of this on nation-wide TV. Our leaders told us that a little nation was being saved, while we watched it being destroyed. As the lie got bigger, the liars got bolder, and soon the press began to report the lies as lies. Hardly a daily newspaper appeared without a report that began: "Administration spokesmen said today, but it is widely known that. . . ."

Politics may have changed little in these years, but the change in political imagination has been momentous. From identification of the real and the ideal to their radical separation. From faith in American institutions to skepticism. From an overconfident zeal to bring a finished American utopia to less fortunate peoples abroad, to a halting retreat in quest of an internal utopia. From Vietnam to LSD. From Peace Corps to pot.

A skeptical political imagination is not necessarily an unhealthy thing. Individuals often go through a kind of Cartesian stage of saying "no" to all their dogmas as preparation for the affirmations of maturity. Perhaps the road to national political maturity is similarly marked. There is no doubt that the effect on the political and social sciences has been liberating. The idols of social value consensus and of the political neutrality of legal institutions have been smashed for good, and the result has been an outpouring of research, bringing us closer to the real ways in which our institutions work.

Philosophical expressions of the skeptical imagination have been slower in coming, but there is little doubt that Robert Paul Wolff's *In Defense of Anarchism* has been perhaps the most well-received attempt to place the skeptical political imagination on a firm philosophical basis. The skeptical political imagination rejects the dogma of the intrinsic morality of the state or its laws. Wolff expresses this by rejecting the notion that the commands of the state are morally binding on its citizens, and he bases this rejection on the primacy of human moral autonomy—the last resource of a skeptical age.

But like many in the generation whose skepticism he expresses, Wolff's defense ends as an inner moral attitude without political direction. Political skepticism is not a political program; it is a personal moral stance. When Wolff tries to translate his defense of political skepticism into a defense of anarchism, he falters, and the discussion becomes obscure. Political skepticism is no more identical with anarchism than religious skepticism is with atheism. Wolff's *denial* that one has a moral duty to obey the state is not the same as the *affirmation* that one has a duty to dismantle the state and replace it with a new form of human association. Indeed Wolff's anarchism entails no affirmation of what one's political duty is, no program for the elimination of the state, and is logically quite compatible with retaining or even strengthening the state. Wolff's anarchism begins as denial and ends as denial. It is the skeptical political imagination chasing its tail.

The skeptical political imagination needs the philosophical underpinning which Wolff has tried to give it, but this is to no avail if it leads nowhere but to inner refusal.

The present essay also begins with the rejection of the notion that the commands of the state are *ipso facto* morally binding on its citizens, but it attempts to go beyond this to indicate that this "rejection" does not—as Wolff would have it—bring us to anarchism and the abandonment of political philosophy. Indeed this "rejection" places even more heavily upon our shoulders the central task of political philosophy: the search for the legitimate state. Hence it is not as a dialectical exercise that the present essay strives to show the limitations of Wolff's analysis, but rather to continue the work of giving philosophical expression to the political imagination of our time. This is a work which should issue, not in an inner moral attitude, but in guidelines by which our institutions can be revitalized according to the wisdom and ideals which do indeed lurk in this generation's imagination.

The present essay makes no claim to complete this work, only to keep it going.

Jeffrey H. Reiman

January, 1972

Introduction

Wolff's Anarchism—the Rejection of the Possibility of the Legitimate State and of Political Philosophy

In a recently published and widely read essay entitled *In Defense of Anarchism,* Robert Paul Wolff argues that the individual's highest obligation is to be morally autonomous, and therefore he is under no moral obligation to obey the laws of any state. If a state is to be considered legitimate, it must have a moral right to rule, which means that its citizens must have a moral obligation to obey its laws. But if the laws of no state are morally binding, then no state is legitimate. *Ergo* anarchism.[1]

Moral autonomy means arriving at one's moral decisions oneself. It means "making the final decisions about what one should do."[2] If, as Wolff would have it, moral autonomy is a man's primary obligation, then a man cannot be under obligation to obey the laws or the commands of the state, because this would allow the state to make the final decision about what he should do. The laws or commands of the state can never be considered more than facts which the morally autonomous man takes into account in determining his moral duty for himself.

1. Robert Paul Wolff, *In Defense of Anarchism* (New York: Harper & Row, 1970), p. 19.
2. Ibid., p. 15.

They can never be considered "as *legitimate,* as having a binding moral force"[3] (emphasis in the original).

Here, then, is Wolff's argument, stripped to the barest bones. If the state is *legitimate,* then its claim to moral authority should be granted. That is, it should be granted the right to make commands which are morally binding on its subjects. If the primary obligation of man is moral autonomy, then he should never accept a claim to moral authority, since granting a claim to moral authority is the same as forfeiting moral autonomy. If no claim to moral authority *should* be granted, then no state is or can be legitimate, "and philosophical anarchism would seem to be the only reasonable political belief for an enlightened man."[4]

For purposes of terminological clarity it should be noted that "moral authority" is my term and not Wolff's. Indeed, from Wolff's standpoint, it is a redundancy, since what I call "moral authority"—the right to give commands which *ipso facto* constitute the moral duty of the person commanded—is for Wolff already included in the meaning of "authority" itself.[5] It should also be clear that "moral authority" entails something stronger than a right to give commands which are merely *prima facie* morally binding, i.e., morally binding in the absence of more compelling moral reasons. Such a right would not be irreducibly in conflict with moral autonomy, since it would not deprive the individual commanded of the right to make the final decision about what he should do. Moral authority, however, is strictly incompatible with moral autonomy, since the former entails the right of one person to create by fiat *the* moral duty of another person, regardless of that other person's decision as to his moral duty. By defining legitimate political authority as moral

3. Ibid., p. 18.
4. Ibid., p. 19.
5. Ibid., pp. 5–9.

authority and by postulating the primacy of the obligation of moral autonomy, Wolff finds an a priori argument against the possibility of political legitimacy in the incompatibility of autonomy and authority. All that is left is anarchism.

But this argument against the possibility of the legitimate state is more than just a defense of anarchism. "The discovery, analysis and demonstration of the forms and principles of legitimate authority—of the right to rule—is called political philosophy."[6] *Wolff's defense of anarchism is equally an attack on political philosophy.* It is an attempt to demonstrate the impossibility of political philosophy by demonstrating that its goal and guiding concept, the "legitimate state" or "legitimate political authority," is a chimera. Wolff's anarchism is the obituary of political philosophy.

It is the purpose of the present essay to argue that this obituary is rather premature, since Wolff's rejection of the possibility of the legitimate state proceeds from a misconception of the nature of political authority and political legitimacy.

Wolff's argument is indeed ingenious. Moral authority and moral autonomy are strictly incompatible. The affirmation of one *means* the rejection of the other. If all authority entails moral authority, then legitimate political authority implies a claim to moral authority. If man's highest obligation is to be morally autonomous, then in principle no claim to moral authority can be justified, and *pari passu* no legitimate political authority can exist. On this foundation Wolff constructs both a defense of anarchism and an attack upon classical democratic theory.

The weak point in this structure is the identification of all authority with moral authority and therefore the treatment of legitimate political authority as a claim to moral authority.

6. Ibid., p. 5.

This conceals a mistaken identification of the political with the moral realm. Starting with the second chapter of the present essay, I will attempt to demonstrate that *political authority is quite distinct from moral authority* and that Wolff's assertion that legitimate political authority implies a claim to moral authority is an arbitrary definitional fiat, corresponding neither to ordinary nor technical usage. In the first chapter I will argue that to define political legitimacy as moral authority is to reduce the legitimate state to absurdity by definition, since *the notion of moral authority turns out on analysis to be a meaningless and unthinkable concept.* The central point I wish to establish is that the affirmation of moral autonomy and the rejection of moral authority in no way lead to the impossibility of legitimate political authority or to the defense of political anarchism.

Wolff fails in the way a mariner who used his compass perfectly would get lost if he misjudged his starting point. He begins by mistaking the moral realm for the political, and from that point he uses his compass perfectly, but he ends up lost because the rejection of *moral* authority is simply irrelevant to the rejection of *political* authority. This irrelevance becomes quite visible as soon as we recognize that the "anarchism" which results from affirming the moral autonomy of the individual and rejecting the moral authority of the state is a personal, inner *moral* attitude—*and not the political doctrine of anarchism at all!*

Traditionally, political anarchism is the doctrine that no state is legitimate, because no state *should* exist. It has been the demand for "the abolition of all political and social coercive institutions within society."[7] Wolff's "anarchism" is the doctrine that no state is legitimate because no state *should* be granted the

7. Rudolph Rocker, "The Ideology of Anarchism," in *The Anarchists,* Irving Horowitz, ed. (New York: Dell, 1964), p. 182; cf. also pp. 15–64 and 74; and Murray Bookchin, "Listen Marxist!" in *All We Are Saying,* Arthur Lothstein, ed. (New York: Capricorn Books, 1971), pp. 122–129.

right to make commands which are morally binding on its citizens. Are these doctrines the same? Is Wolff's anarchism a form of political anarchism? Does Wolff's anarchism imply political anarchism?

I think all these questions must be answered negatively. The best way to see this is simply to ask whether a person who holds that the state's commands are not *ipso facto* morally binding on the individual must also hold that the state should not exist. Obviously not. He might still regard the existence of "political and social coercive institutions in society" as morally preferable to their absence. He might be of so little faith in his fellow men that he believes that without such institutions the human condition would be a war of all against all and that the life of man would be solitary, poor, nasty, brutish—and short. He might quite consistently believe, although the state had no intrinsic right to determine a subject's moral duty, that in fact the state—or a particular state—might be more likely to succeed in getting individuals to perform their moral duties than is likely with forms of voluntary association. He might believe that the function which the state serves is a morally significant as well as necessary function, which cannot be as well served by any other form of institution. In all of these cases, our subject would be locking horns with political anarchists from Bakunin to Goodman—but not with Wolff.

Indeed Wolff's anarchism is not incompatible with the belief that the state *should* exist or with the belief that coercive forms of human association are morally preferable to voluntary forms. *Thus Wolff's anarchism is not incompatible with a rejection of political anarchism.* To put it somewhat crudely, what Wolff fails to see is that the proposition "Everyone *should* determine his own moral duty" (Wolff's anarchism) in no way implies the proposition "Everyone *should* be allowed to do what he determines as his moral duty" (political anarchism). The first proposition is quite consistent with either the affirmation or the denial of the second proposition. Thus, on the question of political liberty, Wolff's anarchism is curiously silent!

This political neutrality of Wolff's anarchism is simply the most visible sign of Wolff's uncritical absorption of political concepts into moral concepts. The affirmation of moral autonomy is not tantamount to the affirmation of political autonomy. The rejection of moral authority is not equivalent to the rejection of political authority. Hence there is no argument from the primacy of moral autonomy to the rejection of political authority, and thus no defense of anarchism. Wolff's argument begins and ends in moral waters, never reaching political shores.

Moral autonomy, as Wolff defines it, is unrelated to coercion —and coercion is the key to the political authority of the state. Indeed, coercion is the key to the meaning of the state, as both political anarchists and libertarians have long recognized. Moral autonomy entails making the final decisions about what one *should* do. Political autonomy entails having the liberty to act upon the decisions one has made. A defense of *political* autonomy can be an argument against coercion, against the authority of the state, but a defense of *moral* autonomy cannot—because one is not *more* morally autonomous when one is *less* coerced. I am not less able to make the final decision about what I *should* do when I *can* do nothing.

Moral autonomy, the rejection of a moral obligation to obey the state, is a subjective negation. It is a purely internal refusal to accept any claim to moral authority. But it is no more. Bound and gagged, one can still make this refusal. It depends not at all on external circumstance, and thus it entails no belief in the moral superiority of one form of human community over another. So long as one rejects any notion of a moral obligation to obey the commands of the dictator, one could be a Wolffian anarchist in the most totalitarian of states. Indeed, were an individual to find that those commands accidentally coincided with the results of his own autonomous moral deliberations, he might live to a ripe old age, a happy and prosperous "anarchist" in the most repressive of dictatorships.

What Wolff misses is that the authority which the state claims is not moral authority but *political* authority—the right to use coercion. And moral autonomy is not incompatible with this right. The moral justification of this right lies in the assessment of the moral consequences of systems of political authority— and this is precisely the kind of task with which political philosophers, including political anarchists, occupy themselves. If this right can be morally justified, then the legitimate state is possible. Which in turn means that there is no a priori argument from moral autonomy to anarchism or to any rejection of the legitimacy of the state. If this much is accepted, then Wolff's attack on classical democratic theory must be subjected to critical re-evaluation.

If political authority is distinct from moral authority, then the moral test of its legitimacy lies elsewhere than in the claim that its commands are morally binding on its subjects. A state can be legitimate without its commands or laws necessarily constituting the moral duty of its citizens. Or, to put it equivalently, an individual can be under a legitimate legal obligation even when he is under a moral obligation to break the law.

For the purposes of this essay, we take the political system and the legal system as roughly equivalent. The law is a uniquely political form of social control; and it is the presence of law which makes a political system a "system." It is not my position that moral inquiry is irrelevant to the consideration of political-legal systems; but rather that it is misguided if it does not start from a recognition of the nature and function of such systems. The issue of the legitimacy of political authority is undeniably a moral issue; but it is a moral issue unique to political-legal systems.

By failing to recognize this, Wolff's attack on the legitimate state is, at its heart, an attack on the relatively independent life of political philosophy itself. It is an attempt to swallow political philosophy up into moral philosophy, which misses the special relationship which does exist between political and moral philosophy. What follows can be characterized as an exploration of this special relationship.

Somewhat more schematically, I will sketch out the main steps in Wolff's argument:

1. _The state is defined by the possession and exercise of authority._ "The state is a group of persons who have and exercise supreme authority within a given territory."[8]

2. _Authority is the putative moral right to command and the right to be obeyed by another person or persons. It entails, thus, both the moral right to command and the moral obligation of those commanded to obey._ "_It must be distinguished from power,_ which is the ability to compel compliance, either through the use or threat of force. When I turn over my wallet to a thief holding me at gunpoint, I do so because the fate with which he threatens me is worse than the loss of money which I am made to suffer. I grant that he has power over me, but I would hardly suppose that he has _authority,_ that is, that he has a right to demand my money and that I have an obligation to give it to him"[9] (emphasis added). "_An authoritative command must also be distinguished from a persuasive argument._ When I am commanded to do something, I may choose to comply, even though I am not being threatened, because I am brought to believe that it is something which I ought to do. If that is the case, then I am not, strictly speaking, obeying a command, but rather ac-

8. Wolff, _Defense of Anarchism,_ p. 3.
9. Ibid., p. 4.

knowledging the force of an argument or the rightness of a pre-scription. . . . *Thus authority resides in persons; they possess it—if indeed they do at all—by virtue of who they are and not by virtue of what they command*"[10] (emphasis added). Au-thority—the right to rule and to be obeyed—is a property of the *source* of a command, not of the *content* of a command nor of the power that backs it up. The adjective *legitimate* is used to distinguish the normative sense of authority from the descrip-tive. That is, to distinguish the moral right to rule and be obeyed, which is truly justified, from those claims to the right to rule and be obeyed which are in fact acknowledged in actual states. Wolff is interested only in the concept of *legitimate authority,* in the question of whether the moral right to rule and to be obeyed can indeed be justified.

3. *The individual's highest duty is to be morally autonomous.* "Every man who possesses both free will and reason has an obligation to take responsibility for his actions . . . when we describe someone as a responsible individual, we do not imply that he always does what is right, but only that he does not neglect the duty of attempting to ascertain what is right."[11] "Since the responsible man arrives at moral decisions which he expresses to himself in the form of imperatives, we may say that he gives laws to himself or is self-legislating. In short, he is au-tonomous."[12]

4. *Legitimate authority is authority which* should *be granted the right to make morally binding commands. But this right con-flicts with the individual's highest obligation, moral autonomy. Thus no individual* should *grant any person or institution the right to make morally binding commands. Therefore, no legiti-mate authority can exist, because there can exist in principle no*

10. Ibid., p. 6.
11. Ibid., p. 13.
12. Ibid., pp. 13–14.

authority which a man should *acknowledge as legitimate. The conflict between autonomy and authority thus yields an a priori argument against the possibility of the legitimate state and for anarchism.* "The autonomous man, insofar as he is autonomous, is not subject to the will of another. He may do what another tells him, but not *because* he has been told to do it."[13] "For the autonomous man, there is no such thing as a command."[14] "The defining mark of the state is authority, the right to rule. The primary obligation of man is autonomy, the refusal to be ruled. It would seem, then, that there can be no resolution of the conflict between the autonomy of the individual and the putative authority of the state. Insofar as a man fulfills his obligation to make himself the author of his decisions, he will resist the state's claim to have authority over him. That is to say, he will deny that he has a duty to obey the laws of the state *simply because they are the laws* . . . he will never view the commands of the state as legitimate, as having a binding moral force"[15] (emphasis in the original). "If all men have a continuing obligation to achieve the highest degree of autonomy possible, then there would appear to be no state whose subjects have a moral obligation to obey its commands. Hence, the concept of a *de jure* legitimate state would appear to be vacuous, and philosophical anarchism would seem to be the only reasonable political belief for an enlightened man."[16]

4a. The a priori status of the claim of the irreconcilability of authority and autonomy is rendered somewhat problematic by the following fact. Wolff does claim that autonomy and authority are reconcilable in *unanimous direct democracy*. But this is a limiting case whose practical improbability renders it effectively

13. Ibid., p. 14.
14. Ibid., p. 15.
15. Ibid., p. 18.
16. Ibid., p. 19.

impossible. One might, with justice, conclude that Wolff has proved not that autonomy and authority are a priori irreconcilable, not that the legitimate state is a priori impossible, but rather that it is *empirically improbable,* i.e., as empirically improbable as unanimous direct democracy is. I think, though, that it is fairer to Wolff's intention to read his conclusion rather in the following terms: autonomy and authority are a priori irreconcilable, the legitimate state is therefore a priori impossible, except in the limiting case of *unanimous direct democracy.* This is a kind of "qualified a priori impossibility," something like the exception which proves the rule.

5. *Deprived of the meaningfulness of its central task, political philosophy loses its claim to independent existence.* Though Wolff never makes this claim outright, it is clear that it is in the balance as he argues. What he calls "casuistical politics as a branch of ethics does exist. It remains to be decided whether political philosophy proper exists."[17] Political philosophy is alternately characterized as the "discovery, analysis, and demonstration of the forms and principles of legitimate authority," and as the attempt to solve the problem of "how the moral autonomy of the individual can be made compatible with the legitimate authority of the state."[18] Since the possibility of success in these tasks is wiped out on a priori grounds, so too is the meaningful possibility of the discipline addressed to them.

6. *Majoritarian democracy, even in the light of its justification according to the social contract theory, cannot claim to be a legitimate form of authority.* "A more serious case for majority rule can be founded on the terms of the contract by which the political order is constituted. . . . On that pact, it is asserted, rests the moral authority of a majoritarian state."[19] "A promise

17. Ibid., pp. 11–12.
18. Ibid., pp. 5, vii.
19. Ibid., p. 41.

to abide by the will of the majority creates an obligation, *but it does so precisely by giving up one's autonomy*"[20] (emphasis in the original). "We appear to be left with no plausible reason for believing that a direct democracy governed by majority rule preserves the moral autonomy of the individual, while conferring legitimate authority on the sovereign. The problem remains that those who submit to laws against which they have voted are no longer autonomous, even though they may have submitted voluntarily. The strongest argument for the moral authority of a majoritarian government is that it is founded upon the unanimous promise of obedience of its subjects. . . . But we have discovered no *moral* reason why men should by their promise bring a democratic state into being, and thereby forfeit their autonomy"[21] (emphasis in the original).

There can be no doubt that Wolff's argument is both provocative and compelling. In response to it I will attempt to establish the following points:

1. Wolff's demand that the state justify a claim to moral authority as the moral test of its legitimacy is meaningless in moral terms. (*Chapter One: The Impossibility of Moral Authority*)

2. The moral test of the legitimacy of the state lies in the moral consequences of the existence of political authority, which is distinct from moral authority and unique to the purposes for which political systems arise. This argument hinges on proving that political authority can be morally justified without having to maintain that that authority *ipso facto* determines the moral duty of its subjects. This much proven, it is clear that political philosophy still exists as a discipline. (*Chapter Two: The Nature of Political Legitimacy*)

3. This moral test of the legitimacy of the state is that which is

20. Ibid., p. 41.
21. Ibid., p. 57.

implicitly recognized by political philosophers in general, and by political anarchists in their rejection of the state. The fact that Wolff does not, indicates the source of the political irrelevance of his anarchism. (*Chapter Three: Political Anarchism versus Moral Anarchism*)

4. Once a state is established as legitimate, there are some moral grounds creating a duty to obey the law. But this is a *prima facie* duty, which can be overridden by other moral considerations. (*Chapter Four: Is There a Moral Duty to Obey the Law?*)

5. Since Wolff has proposed a wrongheaded and impossible test for legitimacy, his claim to have proven majoritarian democracy illegitimate and the social contract theory incapable of providing the principles of legitimate authority must be rejected. I will merely sketch out briefly how the test of legitimacy proposed in this essay might be applied to majoritarian democracy and the social contract theory. (*Chapter Five: Classical Democratic Theory and the Problem of Legitimacy*)

6. Having established that political philosophy can exist as a field of inquiry, I will suggest the proper track for this inquiry, as well as my own suspicion that Wolff's fundamental approach carried with it in advance the danger of a derailment of political philosophy. (*Chapter Six: Finding the Proper Path for Political Philosophy*)

The analysis of the concepts of authority and autonomy and the like can never be more than a preparation for political philosophy and should not be confused with the work of political philosophy itself. Political philosophy begins when we analyze the real conditions of human autonomy and the capacity of forms of political organization to provide those conditions. Purely conceptual analysis of the type Wolff has offered in the first parts of his essay carries with it the danger of mistaking the world of concepts for the world. It is precisely to this danger that Wolff falls prey in defending an anarchism which is politically neutral because it is based on the *concept* of autonomy and not on real human autonomy.

When Wolff begins to speak about real human autonomy in the last chapter of his book, he is no longer talking about the autonomy upon which his defense of anarchism is based. In the first two chapters of his essay Wolff defends a politically irrelevant anarchism based on the concept of autonomy. When in the last chapter of his essay he begins to speak of a politically relevant anarchism, it is not the anarchism he has defended. The slip from Wolff's "moral" anarchism to *political* anarchism reveals the unwisdom of calling the first doctrine anarchism at all, as well as the danger of mistaking the idea of freedom for the concrete political freedom for which men fight and die.

IN DEFENSE OF POLITICAL PHILOSOPHY—

A Reply to Robert Paul Wolff's
In Defense of Anarchism

I. The Impossibility of Moral Authority

> *"What shall I do?" may indeed mean "Tell me what to do." But then I expect you to tell me* what *to do, not to tell me to do something. The first is answering a question, the second is giving orders. In the first case, "What shall I do?" means "What would you do in my place?"; in the second, it means "What are your orders?"*

> *Kurt Baier*
> The Moral Point of View

Wolff has identified the authority of the state with moral authority—the right to make commands which are *ipso facto* morally binding. Hence for Wolff the moral requirement for a state to be legitimate is that it prove its claim to moral authority. Since moral authority is the right to override the individual's moral autonomy, this moral requirement can be equally expressed as a demand for a convincing moral argument establishing a moral obligation on the individual which supersedes his obligation to be morally autonomous. It will be helpful for the reader to keep in mind these two equivalent expressions of *the moral problem* of the legitimacy of the state, according to Wolff.

It is the purpose of the present essay to prove that Wolff has misconceived *the moral problem* of the legitimacy of the state by

failing to see the unique *political* nature of this *moral problem.*
This will be done in Chapter Two. In Chapter One I will argue
that in defining legitimate political authority as moral authority,
Wolff has reduced the notion of political legitimacy to absurdity, by definition. *The justification of moral authority is not
a meaningful moral problem at all!*

My argument in this chapter has three parts:

1. Moral authority is not a meaningful moral concept because
it contradicts the notion of moral obligation itself.

2. The conflict which Wolff poses between moral authority
and moral autonomy is not a meaningful moral conflict. A meaningful moral conflict is a conflict between moral obligations, but
moral authority contradicts the concept of moral obligation,
*and moral autonomy is an essential component of moral obli-
gation.*

3. *Wolff's reconciliation of moral autonomy and moral authority in unanimous direct democracy is as illusory as their
incompatibility.*

A. The Absurdity of "Wild-Card" Moralities

Moral duty, or moral obligation, is the central concept of
morality. A moral duty is a duty to do *what* is moral. Moral
authority, a duty to obey the laws because they are the laws or
the ruler because he is the ruler, implies a duty to do something
not because of *what* it is but because of *where* it comes from.
Underlying this is the mistaken assumption that it is even meaningful to conceive of what we may call a "wild-card" morality.
By this I mean a morality in which a moral obligation to do
something exists, while the nature of that "something" can be
filled in later.

To speak of moral authority, of a right to constitute the moral
duty of another by fiat, of a duty to obey the commands of the

state because they come from the state, to obey the law because it is the law, to obey the commander regardless of his command, to obey the ruler because he is the ruler, is to speak as if someone could hold a moral wild card entitling him to the moral obligation of others to do whatever he determines the wild card to represent. Such moralities generally specify the *source* of the "wild card," God or King or the Law or Father, but these are logically (as well as broadly materially) indifferent to the content that may be given to the "wild card." Since specification of the source does not specify the moral nature of the action to be substituted for the "wild card," *such a morality entails a moral obligation to do an action with indifference to the moral nature of that action,* which is absurd. Since a moral obligation is a duty to do *what* is moral, and that "what" calls for content which can only be filled in by the description of an action which can potentially be shown to be moral, no wild-card morality is thinkable, since it is incompatible with the central concept of morality itself.

It might be countered that a morality of obedience to a ruler is not a wild-card morality in that it does specify *what* one must do, i.e., obey. This assumes several things. First, that the morally most significant aspect of a specific action is that aspect of it which renders it "obeying," i.e., the doing of the action in response to verbal command, etc. But obviously this must be demonstrated for each command, since it would not be possible to demonstrate a priori that the other morally significant features of *any conceivable action* are overshadowed by the actions of obeying. Second, this assumes that the command, "Do what the ruler says!" has the meaning, "Do what is morally right; in this case, it is morally right to obey the ruler." But this is clearly not the meaning of a moral obligation to obey the ruler because he is the ruler or the law because it is the law.

A moral duty to perform an action commanded cannot meaningfully issue from the source of the command any more than a logical "obligation" to believe the conclusion of a sound argument issues from the arguer or an aesthetic "obligation" to see a work of art as beautiful issues from the artist. The moral obligatoriness of an action comes from the nature of the action, just as the truth of the conclusion comes from the nature of the argument and the beauty of the painting comes from the art work itself. To ask for moral grounds outside the nature and consequences of an action for regarding the action as morally obligatory would be like asking for aesthetic grounds other than the aesthetic value of a particular work of art for regarding it as a work of beauty.

The pseudoconcept of moral authority presupposes the meaningfulness of a wild-card morality, since it hinges on a duty *to obey someone,* not a duty *to do something.* This is evident from the fact that moral authority is a quality of the source of the command (the Law, the ruler, or God, for that matter) and indifferent to the content of the command. This is why Wolff says that "authority resides in persons . . . by virtue of who they are and not by virtue of what they command."[1] This is a description of a "wild-card" morality, and since "wild-card" morality contradicts the central notion of morality, *moral authority* is quite literally a *contradictio in adjecto* on a par with round square.

Moral authority—the right to be obeyed, the moral obligation on the part of the one commanded to obey—is patently absurd and impossible on a priori grounds. All of this is implied in the tautology, "a moral obligation is an obligation to do *what* is moral."

No moral obligation to obey law?

It might seem that in throwing out the notion of moral authority we are simply agreeing with Wolff, who, after all, bases

1. Wolff, *Defense of Anarchism,* p. 6.

his defense of anarchism on the rejection of legitimate political authority conceived as moral authority—on the rejection, that is, of any moral duty overriding the individual's duty to be morally autonomous. But our "agreement" with Wolff is based on a profound disagreement. It is more of the coincidence of crossing paths, coming from different starting points and bound for different goals, than of the parallelism of true agreement.

Wolff reaches the impossibility of moral authority starting from an analysis of the qualified a priori impossibility of its reconciliation with moral autonomy and heading toward a defense of anarchism. We reach the impossibility of moral authority starting from an a priori analysis of the concept of moral obligation, headed toward a defense of the *theoretical possibility* (and no more will be ventured) of establishing the legitimacy of political authority. *The difference in the starting points is as essential as the difference in goals.* This difference lies in the fact that had Wolff seen that the concept of moral authority is meaningless, and not merely irreconcilable with moral autonomy, he might have seen that seeking legitimate political authority defined in terms of moral authority is equally meaningless. Had he seen this much he might have hesitated before the unavoidable conclusion that for two and a half millenia political philosophy had been seeking something not elusive, but unthinkable. Such a sobering experience might in turn have led Wolff to seek other grounds for the legitimacy of the state and perhaps to the awareness that his abandonment of political legitimacy and with it, of political philosophy, and his embracing of anarchism, were somewhat premature.

Later we shall question Wolff's identification of legitimate political authority with moral authority. At this point we wish to argue that in claiming to eliminate legitimate political authority by showing the incompatibility of moral authority with the duty of moral autonomy, Wolff has raised a pseudoproblem which infects his whole undertaking. The analysis of pseudoproblems has three pitfalls, and Wolff's analysis has fallen into all three. The first pitfall is the tendency to assume that there is a solution when a solution is as unthinkable as the problem. The second pitfall is the temptation to believe that taking a stand on the solution amounts to a real philosophical stand, while it is no more than unacknowledged recognition or nonrecognition of the pseudoproblem as pseudo. The third pitfall is that of missing the real problem.

Wolff falls into the first pitfall by finding—in his Chapter Two —after all the fanfare about their irreconcilability in his Chapter One—a reconciliation of authority and autonomy, and thus the possibility of legitimate authority in unanimous direct democracy. He falls into the second pitfall by assuming that his rejection of the possibility of legitimate (moral) authority is a real philosophical stand: anarchism—when in fact it is simply a recognition of the tautology: a moral obligation is an obligation to do *what* is moral. He falls into the third pitfall by missing the path which leads to the real arena of political philosophy and the real issues which occupy political anarchists and their theoretical adversaries.

B. The Status of the Duty of Moral Autonomy

Wolff's rejection of legitimate (moral) authority is based on the conflict of authority with autonomy. In other words, since authority entails the moral obligation to obey the person in authority, it necessarily conflicts with the duty of moral autonomy. Indeed, moral authority can be defined as a putative moral obligation overriding the duty of moral autonomy. One can describe Wolff's essay as an attempt to determine whether there are moral grounds for a moral obligation overriding the duty of moral autonomy. Wolff devotes the major portion of his work, the whole of Chapter Two, to analyzing the attempts of democratic theorists to ground just such an obligation. His failure at finding such a ground is, he confesses in his Preface, the source of his anarchism.[2]

But this failure was implicit in the formulation of the problem. There can be moral grounds for a moral obligation overriding a duty to obey a promise or even a duty not to steal. But how could there be moral grounds for a moral obligation overriding the duty of moral autonomy? Such grounds would have to be moral reasons which would persuade the individual that his moral obligation lay in subordinating his moral autonomy to the will of another. But only a morally autonomous individual could entertain moral reasons and be persuaded by them as to his moral obligation. This reveals something extraordinary about the duty of moral autonomy: it cannot be given up on moral grounds because to do so would be a morally autonomous act, and to continue to do so would be to continue to be morally autonomous.

To ask for moral reasons overriding the duty of moral autonomy is to try to rationally persuade someone that he *should* not do whatever he is rationally persuaded that he *should* do. If one succeeds, one fails. This is like me trying to convince you not to be convinced by me. If I win, I lose.

What this reveals is that it is misleading to speak of moral autonomy as *a duty* or as *an obligation*—even if the primary one. Moral autonomy is a component of acting out of moral obligation itself.

To act out of moral obligation means to do what is recommended by the best moral reasons available *because* it is recommended by the best moral reasons available. To neglect to dis-

2. Ibid., p. viii.

cover the best moral reasons is to relinquish the right to claim that one is acting *because* one's act is recommended by the best moral reasons available. Kant saw this quite clearly in noting:

> the distinction between consciousness of having acted *according to duty* [i.e., acting in a way that happens to coincide with the moral law] and *from duty,* i.e., from respect for the [moral] law.[3]

To act out of moral obligation means to scan the situation, size up its moral requirements, evaluate one's alternative courses of action in the light of that situation and those requirements, and to do the act which best fulfills those requirements because it does so. To do less than this may mean that one accidentally or mistakenly does the right thing, or that one's act brings with it the feeling of having done one's duty—but it is not to act out of moral obligation.

A moral obligation is an obligation to do *what* is moral. It is not an obligation to do what one is told is moral, nor what one feels is moral. Hence it implies the necessity of finding out *what* is moral. *To act out of moral obligation it is necessary to be morally autonomous.*

This corroborates our finding that moral authority is chimerical. If it were real, or even possible, it would necessitate a moral obligation overriding moral autonomy. But one could only act on that moral obligation by being morally autonomous.

The duty of autonomy is not *a* duty among others, but intrinsic to the nature of moral duty itself. If this is the case, then the quest for a moral duty to obey authority which might conflict with moral autonomy is the quest for a moral duty conflicting with moral duty itself. It is to ask for a moral obligation in conflict with morality.

One *can* indeed relinquish moral autonomy, as Wolff points

3. Immanuel Kant, *Critique of Practical Reason,* trans. by Lewis White Beck (New York: Liberal Arts Press, 1956), p. 84.

out. But to ask for moral reasons for relinquishing one's autonomy (and this is what it means to speak of moral authority), is not to seek something which merely cannot be found—it is to seek something which cannot be thought. To give up one's moral autonomy is to give up moral obligation, *it is to stop acting on moral reasons. There may be reasons for doing so, but they certainly cannot be moral reasons.* Wolff's "problem" is like that of seeking for scientific reasons for superseding scientific method. These "problems" dissolve as soon as they are clearly formulated.

All that is being said here is that from the moral point of view,[4] the concept of an authority which carries a moral obligation to obey its fiat is impossible. This is because moral autonomy is not an ordinary duty; it is one of the conditions of occupying the moral point of view, and thus a duty to obey a person in whom authority resides is a duty to relinquish the moral point of view. There can be no logically consistent way of even asking for—much less finding—moral reasons conflicting with or superseding moral autonomy. The notion of *moral* authority is a *contradictio in adjecto*.

The simplicity of this argument is hidden by the suggestion that emerges from Wolff's essay that the problem is one of a conflict between two duties in which the moral duty of autonomy reigns supreme over the moral duty of obeying authority, instead of one of simply spelling out the meaning of moral duty itself and showing that there is no meaningful way of speaking of a moral duty of obeying authority.

In what remains of the first section of this paper we shall examine Wolff's claimed success in reconciling autonomy and authority in unanimous direct democracy. This attempt at reconcili-

---

4. Cf. Kurt Baier, *The Moral Point of View: A Rational Basis of Ethics* (New York: Random House, 1965).

ation is as much a sign of Wolff's misconception of the nature of moral authority and moral autonomy as was his analysis of their incompatibility. Wolff has posed the problem of the legitimacy of political authority in terms which render a solution unthinkable.

C. Wolff's "Success" in Reconciling Autonomy with Authority

Wolff writes:

> There is only one form of political community which offers any hope of resolving the conflict between authority and autonomy, and that is democracy.[5]

This already reveals much greater optimism than our argument would allow. But Wolff is not long in waiting for the hoped-for solution.

> There is, in theory, a solution to the problem which has been posed, and this fact is in itself quite important. However, the solution requires the imposition of impossibly restrictive conditions which make it applicable only to a rather bizarre variety of actual situations.[6]

Our argument has demonstrated that a solution, in theory or otherwise, is impossible. And by impossible is meant something quite a bit stronger than the meaning Wolff gives this term when he speaks of an "impossibly restrictive" solution which is still, mysteriously, applicable in actual situations.

> The solution is a direct democracy—that is, a political community in which every person votes on every issue—governed by a rule of unanimity. Under unanimous direct democracy, every member of the society wills freely every law which is ac-

5. Wolff, *Defense of Anarchism*, p. 21.
6. Ibid., pp. 22–23.

tually passed. Hence, he is only confronted as a citizen with laws to which he has consented. Since a man who is constrained only by the dictates of his own will is autonomous, it follows that under the directions of unanimous direct democracy, men can harmonize the duty of autonomy with the commands of authority.[7]

Wolff should read Wolff. A person who "obeys" a command *because* it coincides with his autonomous decision is not obeying authority. If this were not the case, then autonomy and authority could be harmonized in the most repressive dictatorship—should there be an accidental coincidence between the dictator's commands and my autonomous decisions. Surely, as Wolff has already quite ably argued, my complying with a command which coincides with my own autonomous decisions "does not constitute an acknowledgment on my part of any such authority."[8] How could it, if "authority resides in persons . . . by virtue of who they are and not by virtue of what they command"?[9] The harmony of "the duty of autonomy with the commands of authority," which Wolff imputes to unanimous direct democracy, is precisely the external coincidence of autonomy and commands which, Wolff has argued, is no recognition of authority. It would seem that Wolff anticipates this objection when he continues:

> It might be argued that even this limiting case is not genuine, since each man is obeying himself, and hence is not submitting to a legitimate authority. However, the case is really different from the prepolitical (or extrapolitical) case of self-determination, for the authority to which each citizen submits is not that of himself simply, but that of the entire community taken collectively. The laws are issued in the name of the sovereign, which is to say the total population of the community.[10]

7. Ibid., p. 23.
8. Ibid., p. 6.
9. Ibid., p. 6.
10. Ibid., p. 23.

But this is sheer sophistry. The only fact which makes it possible for the citizen in this case to harmonize his autonomy with the commands of authority is the fact that the community's ruling coincides with his own autonomous will. As far as he is concerned, the fact that others agreed with him and thus reached unanimous accord adds not a jot to the "legitimacy" or "authority" of the command. The only member of the community he is obeying because of *who* he is, is himself. He is "obeying" the others because of *what* they command, i.e., because *what* they command coincides with his own decision—not because of *who* they are. Hence he is recognizing no authority (in Wolff's terms) outside of himself, and this means no authority at all.

This becomes clearer as Wolff continues directly:

> The power which enforces the law (should there be any citizen who, having voted for a law, now resists its application to himself) is the power of all, gathered together into the police power of the state.[11]

Let us recall that in addition to distinguishing authority from persuasive argument, Wolff also distinguishes it from "power, which is the ability to compel compliance," not based—as authority is for Wolff—on a right to create a moral obligation to comply. With this borne in mind, it is evident that Wolff's description of the force of the community compelling the recalcitrant citizen to conform to the law he had previously voted for is no reconciliation of autonomy and authority. Moral autonomy entails "making the final decisions about what one should do."[12] Presumably, this is an ongoing responsibility, since one can as well relinquish his autonomy to his own past decision as to another's present decision. Having made a decision yesterday does not relieve me of the duty to reevaluate its wisdom and

11. Ibid., p. 23.
12. Ibid., p. 15.

relevance before acting upon it today. This is clear from Wolff's own critique of the "social contract" theory.[13]

What then becomes of the citizen who votes for a law on one day and then is confronted with it on the next? He must re-evaluate its wisdom and relevance in the present case, or else he neglects "the duty of attempting to ascertain what is right,"[14] which is part of the "duty of autonomy." In reevaluating his previous decision he must rehearse to himself the arguments which persuaded him to vote as he did yesterday, and he will either find these still convincing or no longer convincing. If he finds them still convincing and proceeds upon them to reaffirm his previous decision and act upon it, then he does so not as the result of obedience to authority but rather through recognition of persuasive argument, which Wolff has distinguished from authority.[15] If he finds the arguments no longer convincing, or if he finds new counterarguments which are more convincing, he is duty-bound by the "duty of autonomy" to reject their moral claim on him. If the police power of the collectivity then confronts him and forces him to abide by his previous decision, this is simply an exercise in power, the ability to compel compliance —which Wolff has also distinguished from authority.[16] Hence the relationship of the collectivity to the individual in unanimous direct democracy can be that of either "persuasive argument" or of "power"—it cannot be *moral* authority: no moral obligation to obey is to be found.

There is of course one other alternative. The recalcitrant citizen who previously voted for a law and now resists it may be acting in bad faith. The law may still represent his autonomous decision, though for other reasons (e.g., greed, etc.) he re-

13. Ibid., pp. 41–42. See also, Jean-Paul Sartre, *Being and Nothingness* (New York: Philosophical Library, 1956), pp. 32–33.
14. Wolff, *In Defense of Anarchism,* p. 13.
15. Ibid., p. 6.
16. Ibid., p. 4.

fuses to acknowledge this and to comply with the law. This seems to be the possibility which Wolff has in mind when he continues, in describing the confrontation of the recalcitrant citizen with the power of the unanimous direct democratic state:

> By this means, the moral conflict between duty and interest which arises from time to time within each man is externalized, and the voice of duty now speaks with the authority of law. Each man, in a manner of speaking, encounters his better self in the form of the state, for its dictates are simply the laws which he has, after due deliberation, willed to be enacted.[17]

If it is indeed true that in this situation the individual does recognize that the law represents his duty, then in forcing him to do his autonomously decided duty, the law is still not moving him by authority, by a duty to obey the law simply because it is the law. It is rather, as with persuasive argument, simply the *occasion* for one's recognition and compliance with one's duty.[18] In this case the law and the police power of the state are simply the means by which the individual overcomes obstacles to the doing of his duty, except that now the obstacles are internal.

But this is indeed a fateful turn in the argument, which one would assume Wolff would be reluctant to make. Once it is granted that the state can determine that the disclaimers of the individual as to his autonomous decision are in bad faith and can override those disclaimers to force the individual to do his "internally recognized" real duty, then why have unanimous voting in the first place? The voting might also be in bad faith, and just as legitimately overridden as the later claim to have autonomously changed one's decision. On the principle that the state can determine when the individual's statements as to his autonomously decided duty are in bad faith, autonomy and au-

17. Ibid., p. 23.
18. Cf., ibid., p. 6.

thority can be all too easily reconciled in even the most repressive totalitarian dictatorships.

Finally, it may be replied that as soon as the citizen rejects his previous decision affirming the law, the unanimity is lost, and therefore only so long as unanimity has existed (i.e., is continually affirmed) is there no conflict with autonomy. This is incontrovertibly true. To it must only be added that so long as such continuously affirmed unanimity exists, there is no authority in Wolff's sense of the term. There is no person or institution with the right to create a moral obligation by command. It should also be clear that so long as the legitimacy of a political system is based upon its authoritative decisions coinciding in content with the morally autonomous decisions of its members, no form of authority is possible. This is because the only form this could take is that of unanimous direct democracy with the condition that all individuals have the *continual* right of veto, even to laws they have voted for previously. *This condition means the absence of any form of authority.*

Ultimately, though, Wolff's "success" is a failure because he has failed to see the illusory nature of the quest for a reconciliation of the "duty of autonomy" and the "duty of obedience to authority." He has failed to see that their reconciliation is unthinkable because the "duty of obedience to authority" or of a *moral* authority that could create such a duty is unthinkable. All this follows from a priori analysis of the concept of moral obligation.

In concluding this section, it should be recalled that we have as yet only attempted to demonstrate that Wolff's formulation of *the moral test* of political legitimacy is not a meaningful formulation. We have concurred with Wolff in rejecting the notion of authority as entailing a moral obligation upon the one commanded, to obey. We have called authority defined in these terms *moral* authority. For Wolff, *all* authority is defined in these terms. His defense of anarchism has its source in the assumption that *political* authority is a variety of *moral* authority, and that the rejection of the latter entails rejection of the former, which rejection *is* anarchism. We have argued that *moral* authority is impossible, indeed unthinkable. But we shall argue that *political* authority is something different from *moral* authority, something not rendered impossible even with the revelation that *moral* authority is a *contradictio in adjecto*. Hence the anarchism which Wolff defends is not *political* anarchism. If it is a doctrine of any standing at all, it is a doctrine of *moral* anarchism. We shall utilize these terminological conventions as we turn now to the question of the nature of *political* authority and *political* legitimacy.

II. The Nature of Political Legitimacy

The relation of politics to ethics is not that politics is a branch of ethics. (Neither of course, is ethics a branch of politics.) The plain man recognizes differences between the moral game and the legal game. The philosopher, not unaware of the differences, attempts a reconciliation. He achieves it by interpreting political rules as a sub-class of moral rules, but because his view of morality is itself a narrow one (built up around personal relations as the centre) the effect of this can only be to produce a distorted understanding of political rules.

Thomas McPherson
Political Obligation

A right action may be rationally condemned.

J. J. C. Smart
"Extreme and Restricted Utilitarianism"

We have, in effect, concurred with Wolff in rejecting *in principle* any claim which the state may make to *moral* authority. If we are to make good our defense of political philosophy, we must show that the authority of the state can be legitimate without implying that its commands are *ipso facto* morally binding on its citizens.

In seeking the grounds of political legitimacy, we are not—as Wolff is not—asking for the marks which distinguish the lawful government from the pretenders.[1] This is a legal question. Our question is a distinctly moral question. It seeks the moral reasons justifying the existence of the state, of institutions in which some men rule and enforce their rulings. We are seeking —with Wolff—the moral test which a system of political authority must pass, if it is to be regarded as having a "right to rule," as being legitimate.[2]

I have already indicated that this is a question which must be answered only after we determine the nature and function of systems of political authority. Then and only then can one make the moral judgment as to whether or not this function should be fulfilled, and how well the state—or a particular state—fulfills it.

My argument in this chapter has three parts:

1. Political authority is the right to make commands and use coercion to discourage noncompliance with them.

2. The moral test of legitimacy lies in the moral value of the consequences which a given system of political authority can be expected to produce, in comparison to what can be expected from other systems of political authority or from the absence of such systems.

3. Political authority is distinct from moral authority. The state can have the right to rule without claiming that its commands are *ipso facto* morally binding on its citizens. Wolff's definition of legitimacy is wrong. The legitimate state is possible. Political philosophy lives.

---

1. Cf. R. M. Hare, "The Lawful Government," in *Philosophy, Politics and Society,* 3rd series, ed. P. Laslett and W. G. Runciman (Oxford: Blackwell, 1967), p. 169. Hare distinguishes the legal question of determining the "lawful government" from that of the reasons for giving one's allegiance to a government. Our question is closest to this latter, with the proviso that we are looking only for *moral* reasons.
2. Cf. Wolff, *Defense of Anarchism,* pp. 5, 8.

A. The Nature of Political Authority

Let us start our analysis by tracing Wolff's argument as to the nature of *political* authority. The argument has four steps which we can pinpoint:

1. "The state is a group of persons who have and exercise supreme authority within a given territory."[3]

2. "Authority is the right to command."[4]

3. "Authority is . . . correlatively, the right to be obeyed."[5]

4. Legitimate authority, as opposed to *de facto* authority, "is a matter of the *right* to command, and of the correlative obligation to obey the person who issues the command."[6] Viewing "the commands of the state as *legitimate*" entails viewing them "as having a binding moral force."[7]

We have no quarrel with the first and second points, and the fourth simply distinguishes between *de facto* and *de jure* political authority as defined in the first three. It is the third step which identifies *all* authority with what we have called *moral* authority, with the putative existence of a moral obligation to obey. Thus we must focus our analysis on this third point: does it express something essential to *political* authority?

Let us not be deceived by the fact that all states attempt to engender in their subjects a *feeling* or *belief* that there is a duty to obey the law or the ruler simply because it is the law or he is the ruler. *The question is, is the moral duty to obey essential to the concept of political authority?* We shall argue that it is not.

Wolff corroborates his definition of the state in a footnote reference to a similar endeavor by Max Weber. "Weber empha-

3. Ibid., p. 3.
4. Ibid., p. 4.
5. Ibid., p. 4.
6. Ibid., p. 9.
7. Ibid., p. 18.

sizes the means—force—by which the will of the state is imposed, but a careful analysis of his definition shows that it also bases itself on the notion of authority ('imperative coordination.')"[8] Insofar as Wolff sees Weber as defining the state in terms of "authority" and of "force" as two separate elements of the definition, he misses the unique interconnection of the two which Weber sees, which is central to understanding the unique nature of political authority.

Let us examine Weber's position as found in *The Theory of Social and Economic Organization:*

> An imperatively coordinated corporate group will be called "political" if and in so far as the enforcement of its order is carried out continually within a given *territorial* area by the application and threat of physical force on the part of the administrative staff. A compulsory political association with continuous organization (*politischer Anstaltsbetrieb*) will be called a "state" if and in so far as its administrative staff successfully upholds a claim to the *monopoly* of the *legitimate* use of physical force in the enforcement of its order.[9]

> It is not possible to define a political corporate group, including the state, in terms of the end to which its corporate action is devoted. All the way from provision for subsistence to the patronage of art, there is no conceivable end which *some* political corporation has not at some time pursued. And from the protection of personal security to the administration of justice, there is none which *all* have recognized. Thus it is possible to define the "political" character of a corporate group only in terms of the *means* peculiar to it, the use of force. This means is, however, in the above sense specific, and is indispensable to its character.[10]

The claim of the modern state to monopolize the use of force

8. Ibid., p. 3n.1.
9. Max Weber, *The Theory of Social and Economic Organization*, ed. Talcott Parsons, trans. A. M. Henderson and Talcott Parsons (New York: The Free Press, 1964), p. 154.
10. Ibid., p. 155.

is as essential to it as its character of compulsory jurisdiction and of continuous organization.[11]

Force is essential to Weber's understanding of the noun "state," and the adjective "political." In defining "state," the issue of *legitimacy* first arises in conjunction with the application of force to enforce the order of the state. This is not to say that Weber only speaks of legitimacy with regard to force. He also discusses the legitimate *order* (not in the sense of command, but rather in the sense of a *normative system*),[12] and the bases of legitimate *authority*.[13] With regard to the latter two, he clearly means a system "which enjoys the prestige of being considered binding."[14] The legitimacy of political authority (or "imperative coordination") is based on the legitimacy of a system and on the legitimacy of the use of force to enforce that system. Indeed these are not two different things. The order (system) of the state implies the limits of tolerable behavior *and political authority is the right to use force to establish and maintain those limits.*

The political system represented by a state is the system of the conditions distinguishing acceptable from unacceptable behavior, and thus the conditions under which the state will exercise physical force as a last resort to prevent or punish or discourage unacceptable behavior. *The political or legal system* (and the two are used here interchangeably, in that it is the legal system which makes the political system a "system," i.e., a rule-governed totality as opposed to a simple fact of domination) *of the state can be expressed as the principles specifying when and in what form*

11. Ibid., p. 156.
12. Ibid., p. 124n.48. To avoid any confusion between the sense of order as command and that of order as system, we shall avoid the term "order" and simply use either "system" or "command" when the term comes up in the text or in quotations.
13. Ibid., pp. 324ff.
14. Ibid., p. 125.

force will be applied to coerce behavior into or out of certain forms.

This is corroborated by the anthropologist E. Adamson Hoebel in his analysis of the essential functions which define the law.

> Law performs certain functions essential to the maintenance of all but the very most simple societies.
>
> The first is to define relationships among the members of a society, to assert what activities are permitted and what are ruled out. . . .
>
> The second is derived from the necessity of taming naked force and directing force to the maintenance of order. It is the allocation of authority and the determination of who may exercise physical coercion as a socially recognized privilege-right, along with the selection of the most effective forms of physical sanction to achieve the social ends that the law serves.
>
> The second function of the law—the allocation of authority to exercise coercive physical force—is something almost peculiar to things legal.
>
> Custom has regularity, and so does law. Custom defines relationships, and so does law. Custom is sanctioned, and so is law. But the sanctions of law may involve physical coercion. Law is distinguished from mere custom in that it endows certain selected individuals with the privilege-right of applying the sanction of physical coercion.[15]

To avoid a possible confusion let me hasten to add this note. It is not my purpose to claim that this very brief analysis has put to rest the philosophical issue of whether *the* defining mark

---

15. E. Adamson Hoebel, *The Law of Primitive Man: A Study in Comparative Legal Dynamics* (New York: Atheneum, 1970), pp. 275, 276. "The real situation is that law—the body of rules summed up as law—consists chiefly of rules *about* force, rules which contain patterns of conduct for the exercise of force." Karl Olivecrona, *Law as Fact,* ed. Humphrey Milford (London: Oxford University Press, 1939), p. 134. "Law is the primary norm which stipulates the sanction." Hans Kelsen, *General Theory of Law and State* (New York: Russell and Russell, 1949), p. 61.

of law or legal obligation is the fact of coercion.[16] My claim is simply that whatever else may be required to make the law the law, *a legal system cannot be conceived of without the rule-governed exercise of coercion to back its commands up generally,* even if one can occasionally find a specific law which seems to carry no penalty. None of this suggests that this is enough to characterize the law as legitimate or even as law— simply that it is a necessary condition of the existence of a legal system. This much I trust can be rendered quite consistent with any view of the nature of law.

Based upon this analysis of the political and legal system of the state, reconstructed in somewhat makeshift but I trust not inaccurate fashion from the work of Max Weber and corroborated from that of E. Adamson Hoebel, we can now proceed to specify the nature of *political* authority, which is essential to the concept of the state. *Political* authority is, as Wolff might say, the putative *right to command*. This means in *political* terms the *right* within a given system to give commands which carry with them the threat of physical coercion. *Political* authority is the right to issue commands which will be backed up by physical force to insure behavioral compliance. The form of obligation which corresponds to *political* authority is *legal* obligation.

Political authority is the right to create the objective conditions which will assure objective compliance and discourage or prevent objective nonconformity. The question to be answered is whether this *right,* this *political* authority, can be conceived of as legitimate without having to assume a moral obligation to obey the commands which issue from this authority. This question could be expressed equally well as that of whether *legal*

16. Cf. Lon L. Fuller, *The Morality of Law* (New Haven: Yale University Press, 1969), pp. 108ff; and H. L. A. Hart, *The Concept of Law* (London: Oxford University Press, 1961), chap. 2–6; also H. L. A. Hart, "Legal and Moral Obligation," *Essays in Moral Philosophy,* ed. A. I. Melden (Seattle: University of Washington Press, 1958), p. 98, *inter alia.*

obligation can have moral validity and still be distinct from moral obligation.

B. The Problem of Legitimacy

When we raise the question of the legitimacy of *political* authority, we are asking what distinguishes it from the commands of a gunman, which also carry the threat of coercion in a most immediate form. We are indeed asking, as with Wolff, for the moral justification of this right to command. This question comes in two forms, depending on whether we are questioning a particular command or a whole political system.[17]

When we question the legitimacy of a particular command, we are asking whether it is consistent with the principles that make up the prevailing political system. The political or legal order of the state has been analyzed above as the principles specifying when and in what form force will be applied to coerce behavior into certain forms. Hence the question we will be asking is, does the command in question conform to these principles? Does it threaten force of a type ruled out by our principles (e.g., cruel and unusual punishment, slavery, *peine forte et dure*)? Does it threaten force for purposes which the principles do not entail (e.g., self-incrimination, bill of attainder)? Does it threaten force to prohibit behavior of a type which our system of principles determines is outside the area of behavior which may be coerced (e.g., natural rights, free press, privacy)? All of these questions of the legitimacy of an exercise of authority are summed up in the United States by the question, Is it constitutional?

Now, of course, not all constitutions are of equal value, and

17. Cf. Stephen Edelston Toulmin, *An Examination of the Place of Reason in Ethics* (Cambridge: Cambridge University Press, 1968), pp. 144–52.

not all systems of principles of the conditions of coercion are based on constitutions. Some may be based on custom or tradition. Some may be based simply on the power or influence of a great leader,[18] and thus hardly be systems at all, except insofar as they express the minimal principle that all rulings by the leader are backed by threat of official coercion. This means that in questioning the legitimacy of an exercise of *political* authority one may not be satisfied with finding that it is consistent with the political-legal system of the state. In this case, one will ask a question of a different order. At this point, one must ask *if the system itself is legitimate:* is coercion according to its principles morally justified?

Since this question is indeed *the* moral issue of political systems and *the* problem of political philosophy, let us dwell on some of its possible meanings. At least three candidates come to mind:

1. Will the system in question necessarily always yield moral commands?

2. Will the system in question necessarily always yield commands which are the same moral commands that all its citizens would autonomously give themselves? (This is the question of legitimacy as Wolff uses it in his discussion of unanimous direct democracy; although strictly speaking it cannot be a question of the legitimacy of authority, since if the commands must coincide with those of its autonomous members, this is not authority.)

3. Will the system in question tend to yield more morally worthy results than can be expected from the absence of a political system, or more morally worthy results than—or at least as much as—can be expected from other possible and viable

18. Cf. Weber, *Social and Economic Organization*, p. 328.

political systems? (This, we will argue, is the true question both
of political morality and of political philosophy. It is the real
ground upon which rival political systems and political anarchism
fight their philosophical battles.)

Let us see what can be learned from an analysis of these three
attempts to translate the question of the legitimacy of a political
system.

1. Must a political system always yield moral commands to be legitimate?

The first candidate for the meaning of the question, "Is a
political system legitimate?" fails because it overlooks the fact
that the political system is a *system*.

That is, it is a system of general principles laid down—with or
without provision for orderly alteration—in advance. It is as impossible to ask that a political system always and necessarily
yield moral decisions as it would be to base the validity of the
moral rule prohibiting killing on the assumption that action according to this principle would *always* yield moral results. This
is not a difficulty unique to political systems; it is a difficulty
unique to any general principles which must be applied to particular situations, which can simply never be exhaustively pro-
vided for in advance. One can ask that one follow the most moral
course of action in a particular situation, given the facts available
and the relevant principles. But one cannot ask for principles
which will unfailingly yield the most moral course of action in
any situation unless one decides arbitrarily to define as moral
any course of action yielded by the chosen principles. Short of
this definitional fiat which gives us no way to judge the morality
of different sets of principles, the demand simply can not be
made of a political or legal system.

In recognizing this fact, we perceive something significant
about the nature of the political or legal system which Plato un-

derstood when he spoke of law as "second-best" in the *Statesman.*[19] Plato has the Eleatic Stranger tell the young Socrates:

> the best thing for all is not full authority for laws but rather full authority for a man who understands the art of kingship and has wisdom. . . . Law can never issue an injunction binding on all which really embodies what is best for each; it cannot prescribe with accuracy what is best and just for each member of the community at any one time. The differences of human personality, the variety of men's activities and the restless inconstancy of all human affairs make it impossible for any art whatsoever to issue unqualified rules holding good on all questions at all times. . . . It is impossible, then, for something invariable and unqualified to deal satisfactorily with what is never uniform and constant.[20]

But due to the general paucity of individuals with the requisite wisdom and art to rule unconstrained by law, most states must do with the "second-best." They must design the best laws they can, drawing upon their common experience and expertise and they must punish severely anyone who would transgress the laws.[21]

What the *Statesman* shows us is that in order to have a perfect moral solution in every situation, it is necessary to give someone unlimited power. Once we shrink from giving someone unlimited power, we must give up the possibility of a perfect moral solution in every situation. This truth, somewhat archaically formulated by Plato, expresses the tension between the rule of law and the rule of man.

19. Plato, *Statesman,* ed. Martin Ostwald, trans. J. B. Skemp (New York: The Liberal Arts Press, 1957), p. 72 (297e). On the concept of a legal system, cf. W. Friedmann, *Legal Theory* (New York: Columbia University Press, 1967), pp. 16–18. On the generality of law, cf. Lon L. Fuller, *Morality of Law,* pp. 33ff; and H. L. A. Hart, *The Concept of Law,* p. 21.

20. Plato, *Statesman,* p. 66 (294a–c).

21. Ibid., pp. 71–72 (297b–3), 77 (300b).

Were a man perfectly wise and good, his unconstrained individual rule would yield the moral decision in every particular instance. But given the general scarcity of such lights and the intrinsic difficulty on the part of the populace to judge whether a candidate for such a position of complete power met the qualifications, we prefer to spell out the conditions for the exercise of power in advance rather than let any man rule from beyond the law. Such spelling out in advance must be in general terms. Presumably the loss in individualized justice is made up for by the gains in predictability and the avoidance of the dangers of entrusting unlimited power to someone less than perfectly wise and good. So too, it is hoped that the loss in individualized justice can be diminished—though never in principle eliminated—by designing a legal system with built-in limits, to increase the likelihood that the law will tend toward greater and greater justice in its working. This is the mission and sense of legislative as well as constitutional reform.

Thus, though we can try to design political and legal systems and criticize them so that they tend to produce as systems the greatest justice and the most morally worthy results, we cannot meaningfully ask of them that they necessarily guarantee only moral commands as a condition of their legitimacy.

2. Must a political system always yield commands which are the same moral commands its members autonomously give themselves, to be legitimate?

The second candidate for the meaning of the question, "Is a political order legitimate?" fails because it overlooks the fact that the political system is *political.*

That is, to ask (as Wolff in effect does) that for a political system to be legitimate it must yield commands which are the same moral commands that all its citizens would autonomously give themselves *is to ask that a political system stop being politi-*

cal in order to be legitimate. It is to overlook the nature of politics and the situations in which the need for political systems arises. Politics, as already noted by Weber, is identified with force or with the power to enforce one's will. Political discourse arises in response to the recognition of the fact that such power exists wherever human beings congregate, that it is fraught with danger and that ways must be found to control it. As soon as one looks for ways to control power, he looks for forms of power to control power. That is, he attempts to distinguish legitimate from illegitimate uses of coercion so as to deal with the otherwise uncontrolled power that exists as a fateful potential wherever men congregate.[22]

What this means is that political systems *begin* from the *assumption* that some areas of behavior are too crucial to the mutual well-being and survival of the community to be left to the consciences of its members. Some behaviors must be met with force, because the dictates of each man's conscience are not sufficiently trustworthy to leave each man wholly free to do the behavior he chooses to do.

Political systems cannot, in principle, be *wholly* in conformity with the actual autonomous decisions of their members except by accident. As our analysis of Wolff's "success" with unanimous direct democracy has shown, to make the *principle* of a political system conformity with the individual autonomous decisions of its members, is to eliminate it as a *political* system. Political systems start from the assumption that some forms of behavior must be prevented, even if they are conscientiously chosen.[23] *This is the logic of political systems.*

22. Cf. Hoebel, *Law of Primitive Man;* Dennis Lloyd, *The Idea of Law* (London: Penguin, 1964), p. 43; Edwin M. Schur, *Law and Society: A Sociological View* (New York: Random House, 1968), pp. 72–75.

23. It is clear that this is the logic of the criminal law in excluding motive from the definition of criminal conduct. Cf. Jerome Hall, *General Principles of Criminal Law,* 2d ed. (New York: The Bobbs-Merrill Company, 1960), pp. 93–104.

They can be designed so as to tend to greater or lesser conformity with what morally autonomous individuals can be expected to decide—by incorporating popular consent into the legislative process, by determining some areas of action as beyond legal intervention (e.g., religion, speech, etc.), or by determining what acts are truly harmful and must be prevented and ridding the law of entrenched prejudice and immorality,[24] etc. But they cannot have, *as their principle and starting point,* conformity to the actual autonomous decisions of their members, and remain *political.* To hold otherwise would be to assume that "there might be a political society without political obligations, which is absurd. For we mean by political society, groups of people organized according to rules enforced by some of their number."[25]

This insight seems also to be lurking in Plato's *Statesman,* although one must take Plato's words beyond their immediate intention. Because of the difficulties of finding and recognizing a good and wise man to grant unlimited power, we adopt a system of laws as a "second-best" way to govern society. If an all good and wise man could rule without laws, a society of all good and wise men could rule themselves without laws. But this is necessarily harder to find than one good and wise man, since "in no state whatsoever could it happen that a large number of people received this gift of political wisdom which would enable them to govern the city by the pure intelligence which would accompany it."[26]

24. Cf. Edwin M. Schur, *Crimes Without Victims: Deviant Behavior and Public Policy* (New Jersey: Prentice-Hall, Inc., 1965).

25. Margaret Macdonald, "The Language of Political Theory," in *Logic and Language,* ed. Anthony Flew (Oxford: Blackwell, 1960), p. 184; also Baier, *Moral Point of View,* p. 68. "To speak of regulations makes sense only because they may or may not be in force. For them to be in force presupposes the whole social apparatus of rule-enforcement. There could be no regulations in a world of hermits. . . ."

26. Plato, *Statesman,* p. 71 (297b).

Hence, once again, and perhaps with even greater reason, we are left with second-best: a system which lays down in advance and in general terms the forms of behavior which will be tolerated and those which will be dealt with forcibly, the areas in which commands may be made that will be backed up with force. Of course, Plato would never allow us to give up trying to design our political and legal order in the way most like the perfect constitution.[27] For our purposes, this may mean most like the laws which morally autonomous individuals would give themselves.

The question of the legitimacy of a political system cannot strip it of precisely that which makes it political. It must start from a recognition of the logic of political systems, which arises from their unique function. Political and legal systems arise in response to the fact of power in human communities, and to the assumption that individual conscience or moral autonomy is not an adequate safeguard against the exercise of that power by some to the detriment of others or to the community as a whole. Without the *fact* of power, and the *assumption* that individual conscience is an inadequate control, there would be no such thing as a *political* system. Hence *the starting point of a political system is the fallibility of conscience.*[28] *The function of a political system is to provide, by means of physical force, the safeguard that individual moral autonomy apparently cannot.*

Now, in questioning the legitimacy of a political system one can ask if the system fulfills this function and if it fulfills it with the least possible sacrifice of the values for which men live in communities—or, one can ask whether the assumption that a political system is necessary to provide the safeguard that conscience cannot is a valid assumption. The former questions spring from the fact that some political systems simply monopo-

27. Ibid., pp. 71–72 (297 c–e).
28. Cf. Hall, *Criminal Law,* p. 95.

lize the arbitrary exercises of power they claim to prevent, and some achieve security at the price of freedom and privacy and trust. The latter question is indeed the issue which separates anarchists from defenders of political systems but—and this is central to this essay—*this is not the question Wolff raises.*

3. Is the question of the legitimacy of a political system that of whether it will tend to yield more morally worthy results than can be expected from the absence of a political system, or more morally worthy results than—or at least as much as— can be expected from other possible and viable political systems?

We have already found enough, in rejecting the first two candidates for the meaning of the legitimacy of a political system and of the political authority based upon it, to answer this question in the affirmative.

Our discussion of the first two possibilities has netted us two points which are essential in considering the legitimacy of a political system:

1. It is essential to bear in mind that a political system is a *system*. That is, it is a system of general principles expressing the conditions under which coercion may be utilized to prevent or punish or otherwise discourage unacceptable behavior. It must be judged as only a system of general principles can be judged, in terms of their general foreseeable effects. A system of general principles cannot be held up to a standard of perfect moral results, except as a model toward which to aspire. Rather, a system of general principles must be compared in its generally expected effects with other systems and with the effect generally expected from the absence of such systems.

2. It is essential to bear in mind that a political system is *political*. That is, it begins from the assumption that individuals' consciences are fallible and thus not a sufficient safeguard against

see Wolff

Wolff's definition of "political"?

the abuse of power, and thus that some forms of official coercion must be used to prevent certain types of behavior. Hence the question of the legitimacy of political systems must not, *in advance and by definition,* negate the function and logic of political systems.

This is, of course, not to determine *in advance and by definition* that the political function is essential to legitimacy. This would be to do to political anarchism what Wolff does to political systems in the name of moral anarchism. This would be to define legitimacy as the legitimacy-of-systems-of-coercion, to incorporate into the definition of legitimacy the assumption underlying political orders: that some form of officially exercised coercion is necessary to human society. Such a definition of legitimacy would rule anarchism out of the running precisely the way Wolff's definition of legitimacy as morally binding on the individual or as compatibility with individual moral autonomy rules political systems out of the running. Either definition of legitimacy would be equally arbitrary.

Rather, the definition of legitimacy must be a priori neutral on the question of the necessity of official coercion. It must thus entail the possibility of comparing communities with political systems with one another and with communities without political systems. The only morally relevant way in which this comparing can take place is in terms of the moral value of the results which can be expected from the various forms of community which are being compared. This is the only rational way in which one can ask for the moral justification of the existence of the state— or any particular state. Since the state is defined by the possession of political authority and political authority by the claim to a right to rule and enforce its rulings, it follows that if the existence of a state is morally justified, then its right to rule is *eo ipso* morally justified. A state whose claim to a right to rule has been morally justified must be a *legitimate* state.

This formulation delineates the task and the boundaries of that mode of discourse properly called *political philosophy*. It does, as Wolff's formulation does not, make sense out of the debates between liberals and Marxists, libertarian socialists and totalitarians, and between all of these and those who maintain that political orders are unnecessary, even detrimental, to the human functioning of human communities—the *political* anarchists. Needless to add, political philosophy is alive and well.

At this point it might be objected that if we could successfully prove that the existence of a state is morally justified, does that not imply that the commands of the state define the moral duty of its citizens? In other words, when all is said and done, isn't political authority still a form of moral authority?

Here is the keystone of our defense of political philosophy. *We must demonstrate that political authority can be legitimate, i.e., morally justified, while neither actually nor putatively coinciding with the individual's moral duty.* Since legal obligation corresponds to political authority, we could equally well characterize this as a demonstration that legal obligation could have moral force distinguishing it from a command backed merely by threat of penalty and still not coincide with the individual's moral obligation.

If we succeed in this, it must be abundantly clear that there is no a priori argument from moral autonomy to anarchism or to the rejection of the legitimate state or to the obituary of political philosophy.

C. Does Legitimate Political Authority Entail a Moral Duty to Obey Its Commands?

Wolff's argument proceeds from moral autonomy to the rejection of moral authority to the rejection of legitimate political authority to the defense of anarchism. The weakest link in this chain is that which connects the rejection of moral authority to the rejection of legitimate political authority, since this is based on the assumption that political authority is a form of moral authority. If we can break this link, the chain upon which Wolff hangs his defense of anarchism is broken.

I have indicated, thus far, the unique nature of political authority and the moral test of its legitimacy. To complete this project, it must be demonstrated that political authority can pass this moral test, can be legitimate, and still not be morally binding on the citizen. With this, legitimate political authority is distinguished from moral authority, and the link between moral autonomy and anarchism is clearly sundered.

Of course it cannot be denied that ordinary usage sees a connection between the legitimacy of the state and the citizen's moral obligation to obey its laws. In Chapter Four we shall have occasion to delineate the sense in which conventional usage is accurate in registering such a connection. At no point does that connection even approximate Wolff's conception of it as a moral obligation overriding the individual's own autonomous moral judgment. I will argue that the true connection between legitimacy and moral obligation is that of a general overlap without a complete coincidence, and that legitimacy suggests *prima facie* reasons for obedience, which can be overridden by other moral considerations. In no way does this constitute a moral obligation overriding individual moral autonomy. It constitutes, rather, moral reasons which ought to enter into the deliberations of a morally autonomous individual when he is determining whether or not to obey the law.

No such limited and conditioned moral obligation to obey is implied in Wolff's definition of legitimacy. If it were, then there would be no conflict with moral autonomy. Rather, for Wolff, legitimate political authority, if it means anything, means the right to create moral obligations for individuals overriding their moral judgments. It means a total coincidence between the commands of legitimate political authority and an individual's moral duty—no matter what he thinks. Implicit in Wolff's argument, indeed *necessary* for his argument, is the assertion that every legitimate law of a legitimate authority constitutes *the moral duty* of the individual to whom it is addressed. For Wolff, there appears no alternative between this and the notion of law as a nonmoral command backed by threat of force. This is clear from Wolff's treatment of the gunman situation.

> When I turn over my wallet to a thief who is holding me at gunpoint, I do so because the fate with which he threatens me is worse than the loss of money which I am made to suffer. I grant that he has power over me, but I would hardly suppose that he has *authority,* that is, that he has a right to demand my money and that I have an obligation to give it to him[29] (emphasis in the original).

The right to demand my money and my obligation to give it up travel together in Wolff's analysis. What the legitimate authority has a moral right to demand, I have a moral obligation to give. Here is the confusion of moral authority with political authority. This confusion is based on the assumption that it is absurd to think that the state might have a moral right to demand something of me when I do not have a moral obligation to give it. It is based on the assumption that it is unthinkable that the state might have the moral right to coerce my compliance with its command when my moral obligation lies precisely in refusing compliance.

Wolff's identification of moral authority and political authority is based on the assumption that it is nonsensical to imagine a law being legitimate, i.e., morally justified, which an individual did not have a moral obligation to obey. The assumption that if a law is legitimate it must constitute the moral duty

29. Wolff, *In Defense of Anarchism,* p. 4.

of the citizen, implies that the moral reasons which may compel us to legislate a law must also be reasons which compel us to obey that law. This overlooks the fact that the decision to legislate a law or not is a decision made under different circumstances and promising different consequences than the decision to obey a law or not. In somewhat oversimplified terms, the decision to obey or disobey is made by one individual *for* himself in response to a specific present situation, the factual details of which are largely readily at hand. The decision to legislate or not is made by an individual or individuals acting in the name of the community *for* the whole community in response to future situations which can only be foreseen in a most general fashion. It should be obvious that there will be factors morally relevant to the first decision which are largely irrelevant to the second and vice versa. For instance, and still in oversimplified terms, the legislator—mobilizing the organized power of the community and addressing himself to the acts of as yet unspecified individuals—is much more dependent for the moral validity of his decisions upon broad generalizations about the nature of men's motives and actions than is the individual deciding whether or not to obey a law. The individual driver's decision to disregard the legal speed limit is a decision of a different order, based on different facts and leading to different consequences than the decision to set the legal speed limit or the legal penalties for speeding or the legal conditions under which disregard of the speed limit will not be penalized, for all drivers. Thus Wolff's identification of legitimate political authority with moral authority is based upon a mistaken assumption: that of a pre-established harmony between the moral justification for laws and the moral justification for individual actions. *This is the kernel of Wolff's confusion of the political and moral realm.*

In responding to this I will draw upon the analysis of the nature of political authority and the moral test of legitimacy to prove that the laws of a state can be legitimate without coinciding with the individual's moral duty. *The moral justification for a law is not the same as the moral obligation to obey the law,* although there are good reasons for expecting them to largely overlap.

If a law with its threat of coercion can be morally justified, this means that one is under a legitimate legal obligation to obey it. This is what is lacking from the gunman's command with its threat of coercion. But this legal obligation, though not without moral force, is not the same as *the* moral obligation of the citizen. It is simply one morally relevant factor figuring in his determination of his moral obligation.

To prove this, it is necessary to show how a law with its threat and use of coercion can be truly morally justified even while a citizen's true moral obligation dictates disobedience. This becomes clear as soon as it is seen that the maxim upon which the individual determines his moral duty is different in principle from that which validates the moral right to issue laws and use coercion to discourage noncompliance with them. These maxims are not only different; they can in principle lead to conflicting conclusions which are both true.

In the broadest terms the maxim which determines the individual's moral duty in any particular case is the obligation to choose and perform that act which he reasonably expects will be most productive of morally valuable results. One might go further to determine what is meant by "morally valuable" in this statement, but this is not necessary for our purposes. Even with this seemingly tautological formulation, we will be able to see the difference between the maxim upon which the individual determines his moral duty and that upon which the community determines its moral right to coerce obedience.

Recalling our discussion of the nature of *political* authority, the maxim which determines the moral right to use coercion to prevent certain behaviors can be formulated in terms of the following question: Recognizing the fallibility of men's consciences, what will be the effect on the community of incorporating the principle of placing no coercive control on the behavior in question beyond the moral sense of the actor, in comparison to the effect on the community of incorporating the principle that physical coercion will be used to prevent or discourage such behavior regardless of the moral sense of the actor?

It is easy to see that the maxim determining the individual's moral duty and that determining the state's right to use coercion may lead to conflicting conclusions, *both of which may be quite correct.* And it is precisely this fact which indicates that political authority can be legitimate even when it conflicts with the individual's moral duty. Thus political authority can be legitimate without being morally binding on its subjects.

Let us examine a rather extreme example which brings out the relevant principles. An individual in a community may, by investigating the facts of the situation and estimating the various consequences of the actions to choose from, determine that it is his moral duty to assassinate an evil member of the community. *Let us assume throughout this discussion that he is correct in reading this as his moral duty.* (Pacifists may find this too much to tolerate. They are invited to substitute something less offensive, like physically restraining or confining the evil member, or stealing from the rich to give to the poor. The same principles will apply.)

What *should* the community's response be? Should it try to determine whether or not the individual is *sincerely* acting out of his sense of moral duty? Or whether or not the individual is *correct* in his reading of the nature of his duty? Should it make punishment conditional on either the finding that the individual has acted in bad faith or in ignorance of his true moral duty? Before the community can do this, it must determine what the effect will be of its acting upon the principle: Killing done out of a sincere sense of moral duty, or even out of a sense of moral duty that turns out to be correct, will not be punished. It must compare the reasonably foreseeable effects of this principle with that of applying coercion to prevent killing regardless of the motive.

It must compare the reasonably foreseeable nature of life in a community in which the taking of a life were simply a matter of individual conscientious judgment or in a community in which a citizen knew that he would only be punished for taking a life if his conscientious judgment had been incorrect, with the nature of life in a community in which everyone knew that all killing—regardless of motive or conscientious judgment— would be severely punished. Though there is no question but that each of these arrangements might have advantages impossible in the others, the question which must be addressed is, which arrangement is morally superior on the whole? Is it better for the community in general and over the long run that its members know that killing is simply a matter of individual moral judgment for which no official punishment is to be expected, or that killing will only be punished when the individual's moral judgment has been incorrect, or that killing will be punished even when the individual killer is quite sure that he is doing the right thing?

Let us keep the existential situation in mind. The community cannot avoid responding to the individual killer in a way which will influence the future choices of other individuals. The community cannot avoid acting in a morally fateful way. Even if it ignores the killing, this ignoring will have its consequences. Indeed, the whole stretch of possible community responses, from ignoring the killing to executing the killer and his family, will have consequences for the future expectations, decisions and actions of as yet unspecified individuals. To the extent that these consequences can be reasonably foreseen, the community cannot avoid moral responsibility for them. It is then an empirical question as to whether we can expect enough people to misjudge their situation or their moral duty so that a law with a proviso granting immunity from punishment for those who kill out of a sense of moral duty or out of a correct sense of moral duty will lead to more or less immoral taking of life than a law punishing murder without such a proviso. If we accept that the moral justification of a law punishing murder hinges on such an empirical question, then we accept in principle the possibility of a morally justified, i.e., legitimate, law which can conflict with the individual's moral duty.

Presumably, in our example, recognizing the fallibility of human conscience, it will be determined that it is morally preferable to use coercion to discourage killings, regardless of motive, than not to do so. Admitting that this may sometimes lead to less than perfectly moral results, e.g., when, as in our example, it is conceded that the individual has correctly judged his moral duty to be the taking of a life, it is generally agreed to be a net gain morally to have a system which backs up the command not to kill with the threat of coercion.[30] Even if one argues that individuals' consciences are sufficiently trustworthy to be left to make this decision in the absence of coercion, one has recognized that it is at least *in principle* possible to justify the use of coercion in these terms. This means that it is in principle possible to morally justify the use of coercion to enforce a command without having to imply a moral duty to obey the command. This means that a system of political authority or a law can be

30. Cf. Hall, *Criminal Law,* pp. 93–104. "For it is impossible to forbid any class of harms without including rare marginal instances where a maximum of good motivation combines with the minimum of proscribed harm, or even no harm at all, so that the final estimate is that the value protected by the rule was not impaired in the instance." Hall, *Criminal Law,* p. 94.

legitimate, can be morally justified, whether or not one is in every instance morally bound to obey. Hence Wolff's identification of legitimacy with the morally binding force of the law is incorrect, if the legitimacy of political authority means the moral justification of its existence. And it can mean nothing else.

There is another way in which this can be brought out. The assumption that political authority must be morally binding on the individual if it is legitimate, i.e., morally justified, implies that when a command of the state conflicts with an individual's moral judgment, if the command is legitimate, then the individual's moral judgment must be wrong. That is, if legitimate law is taken as spelling out the individual's moral duty, then when he judges that his duty is contrary to legitimate law, the individual *must* be mistaken. But the legitimacy of the law does not imply that the individual moral judgments with which it may conflict are wrong. The moral justification for political authority, for the law, lies in the belief (an empirical assertion capable of confirmation or disconfirmation) that some areas of human behavior are too risky to be left to individual moral judgment. This in no way implies that individual moral judgments will always be wrong in these matters. Indeed, it is not incompatible with the assertion that they will sometimes be correct. It is based rather on the belief that individual moral judgment will be wrong *frequently enough* so that it will be better on the whole to prevent or discourage the free exercise of individual moral judgment in these areas of behavior than to allow its unhindered expression. To the extent that this belief can be established as true for a political-legal system, to that extent is the political-legal system *legitimate*.

Thus it is quite conceivable that a command of the state is legitimate, even though it conflicts with my correct judgment as to my moral duty in a particular situation. It is quite conceivable that I find myself under a legitimate legal obligation, and at the same time find that my moral obligation dictates that I disobey the law. This does not in any way reduce the commands of the law to the commands of a gunman writ large. This in no way renders either legal or political authority mere facts of power without moral legitimacy.

Wolff identifies legal obligation with moral obligation, and therefore political authority with moral authority, because he sees no alternative for "legal obligation" outside of either a) the gunman's command merely backed up with the threat of force, or b) a command which I am morally obligated to obey. He fails to see that what the law has, and the gunman lacks, is the morally justifiable right to use the threat of force to compel my compliance. *And this right can be morally justified without the assumption that I am morally obligated to obey.*

Since the moral justification for the use of force to compel compliance in some areas of behavior lies in the general consequences of allowing such behavior to exist unhindered versus those of dissuading such behavior through the use or threat of force, it will usually be the case that the moral justification for a legal command and an individual's moral duty will overlap. Thus it is to be expected that morally justified legal obligations will largely overlap with true moral obligations, or that it will be extremely difficult to morally justify legal obligations which generally and for the most part conflict with individual moral obligations. But none of this entails a necessary coincidence of legal and moral duty.

What is meant by saying that the individual confronts a morally justified (or *legitimate*) legal obligation is no more than that he confronts a command—issuing from a duly constituted representative of the state—which is backed up with the threat of penalty, *and* that the existence of commands of this type with their accompanying sanction is morally preferable to their absence. Precisely because legal commands can only be justified at a level of some generality, these commands may or may not coincide with an individual's moral duty in the particular instance.

I can recognize that it is morally preferable for the state to prohibit acts of the type I am about to perform, even though my moral duty dictates that I perform it. The state may be right in using coercion to prevent me from committing an act, even if I am right in determining that this act constitutes my moral duty. Indeed, this is precisely what is meant by saying that my legal obligation conflicts with my moral obligation. It would be impossible to say this if political authority and moral authority were the same.

Our argument is that a legal decision to punish an act can be legitimate, and an individual's decision that it is his moral duty to do the act be correct, without contradiction. Hence Wolff is wrong in assuming that for a state to be legitimate, its commands must be morally binding on its citizens.

It should be obvious of course that the moral test of the state's right to use coercion in a particular instance dovetails with the test of its legitimacy as a political system as a whole. *Thus it is clear that the state can be legitimate and in conflict with my moral duty.* It is precisely because this conflict is possible—not inevitable, perhaps not even usual—that such a thing as legitimate political authority exists: the right to command with the right to exercise force to bring about compliance with its command, regardless of what my conscience dictates to me as my moral duty.

There can be authority only where there can be conflict between a command and an individual's autonomy. Such authority cannot be *moral* authority, i.e., a moral duty superseding the individual's moral autonomy, since, as we already saw, the individual can only act upon a moral duty if he is morally autonomous. But this authority can be *political* and morally justified along lines different from those which create an individual's moral duty in a particular situation. That is, authority can be *political* if it proceeds from the assumption that the behavior in question is too dangerous to leave up to individuals' autonomous moral decisions. And, that *political* authority can be *legitimate* if the assumption which makes it *political* is correct, given the available knowledge. This is what distinguishes legitimate legal obligation from the gunman's command, without coalescing legal obligation into moral obligation.

Thus it is quite reasonable to think of *political* authority as something quite different from *moral* authority, sharing with the latter the claim to a right to command but not the claim to a right to create a moral duty to obey its commands; and making a claim which *moral* authority does not essentially make, that of a right to use coercion to compel compliance with its commands.[31] Strictly speaking, the claim that a law or the legal system is legitimate *in principle* can never relieve a man of the moral decision as to whether he should obey the law or disobey it and risk the consequences. The individual may indeed acknowledge the legitimacy of the law, recognize the moral superiority of sanctioning the behavior in question over leaving it to individual conscience. The same individual may quite consistently determine that his moral duty lies in disobeying the law at this time in this situation.

Wolff is simply wrong in assuming that for political authority to be legitimate, its commands must in every instance have "a binding moral force" on the individual, although if the state is

31. "Consider the law . . . as what might be termed a *choosing* system, in which individuals can find out, in general terms at least, the costs they have to pay if they act in certain ways." H. L. A. Hart, *Punishment and Responsibility* (New York: Oxford University Press, 1968), p. 44; also Fuller, *Morality of Law,* p. 25.

legitimate then it is to be expected that its commands will generally and in the long run coincide with its citizens' real moral obligations.

Political authority can be distinguished from moral authority —even though actual states may attempt to engender in their subjects a feeling or belief that one is morally bound to obey political authority. Rather, *political* authority seeks its legitimacy in terms unique to the concerns which generate political organization.

Distinguished in these terms, we see that *it is the rejection of political authority and not moral authority which distinguishes political anarchism as a political philosophy.* In spite of Wolff's claims that he is speaking of anarchism as a "political doctrine" and as a "mode of social organization,"[32] his anarchism is not a political philosophy at all. Since it is a rejection of moral authority and not of political authority, it is no more than a description of one of the conditions of acting upon moral obligation.

32. Wolff, *Defense of Anarchism*, pp. 18, viii.

III. Political Anarchism versus Moral Anarchism

> *For the anarchist, freedom is not an abstract philosophical concept, but the vital concrete possibility for every human being to bring to full development all capacities and talents with which nature has endowed him, and turn them to social account. The less this natural development of man is interfered with by ecclesiastical or political guardianship, the more efficient and harmonious will human personality become, the more will it become the measure of the intellectual culture of the society in which it has grown.*
>
> Rudolph Rocker
> "The Ideology of Anarchism"

> *. . . anarchists . . . believe in a moral progress such that the social casing of coercion may eventually be discarded, leaving a matured, self-respecting humanity to maintain freely its order and character. They believe, further, that the gradual decrease of state pressure would hasten this event, because human nature has a bent to goodness, and gives the best account of itself when unfettered by artificial requirements.*
>
> William Ernest Hocking
> "Anarchism and Consent"

The belief in the possibilities of life unhampered by
instruments of coercion reveals the rationalistic
bias of most forms of anarchism in the exaltation
of human reasonableness and goodness, and
contempt for the irrationality of the State.

Irving L. Horowitz
"A Postscript to The Anarchists"

I have suggested that *political* anarchism is the doctrine that no state is legitimate because no state *should* exist. I have further argued that the moral test of legitimacy lies in the moral consequences of the existence of political authority. Wolff has taken the test of legitimacy to be the ability to establish on moral grounds the morally binding quality of the state's commands. The reader is invited to peruse the literature of anarchism to determine for himself (quite autonomously) which is the test which the theorists of anarchism use when they demand the abolition of the state.

I believe that the reader will find that political anarchism takes the following general form: The natural condition or potential of man is extolled as being of such quality that his most human and brotherly qualities flower in the absence of coercive institutions. Thus coercive institutions are at once unnecessary to maintain peace and actually destructive of the finest qualities of human life. In short, they produce more evil than they combat. Hence, no state can be legitimate, because there is no moral justification for any coercive institution's existence.

If the anarchist decries the state in the name of freedom, it is in the name of liberty, the freedom from coercion, not in the name of any inner freedom or moral autonomy. The freedom which is defended is real, concrete freedom, which the anarchist maintains is most humanely nurtured in the absence of coercion.

In any event, the anarchist implicitly accepts the effects of forms of human association on individuals and on the community as the proper locus for their justification or condemnation. The political anarchist shares with other political philosophers the belief that the values for which men congregate —community, security, love, aid, exchange of things and ideas— are the standard against which all or any social institutions must be tested. He argues that systems of political authority are simply less conducive to those values than is their absence. He argues that the assumption upon which political systems rest—that individual autonomy is not a sufficient safeguard on the abuse of power in the human community—is incorrect.

The anarchist accepts implicitly a standard of legitimacy that *could in principle* be achieved by the state. He just argues that in actuality it does not and will not achieve that standard. Hence, he does not argue, as Wolff does, against the possibility of legitimacy on a priori grounds or against the possibility of political philosophy.

The Frenchman Pierre-Joseph Proudhon, the first man to call himself an anarchist, "held government responsible for disorder and believed that only a society without government could restore the natural order and recreate social harmony."[1] In positive terms, anarchism refers to the "condition of being unruled because rule is unnecessary for the preservation of order."[2]

> The same belief that, if individuals are left to pursue their natural desires, general benefit will be the result, is present in anarchism as in early liberalism. However, while the liberal doctrine has been qualified by the admission that some social authority is necessary to lead the "invisible hand" and to see to it that the "natural" laws are not tampered with, anarchism refuses to accept such an admission. . . . The anarchists deny

1. Daniel Guerin, *Anarchism: From Theory to Practice* (New York: Monthly Review Press, 1970), pp. 11–12.
2. George Woodcock, *Anarchism: A History of Libertarian Ideas and Movements* (Cleveland: World Publishing Company, 1962), p. 10.

the necessity of government *because of their belief*—which most nonanarchists will dismiss as utopian—*that the dictates of reason, or the social instincts of human nature, or both, if unhampered by external coercion, will secure free, harmonious social life*[3] (emphasis mine).

The key to these statements is that they accept the *moral results of a social system as the proper test of its legitimacy.*

Because Wolff does not accept this as the proper test of legitimacy, his doctrine leads to no judgment as to whether or not the state—or any coercive institution—*should* exist. His is a purely internal refusal to accept the state's commands as *ipso facto* morally binding—but it leads to no commitment to replace coercive institutions with voluntary ones.

I have referred to those who hold that political orders or systems of official coercion are unnecessary or detrimental to the human community as *political* anarchists, to distinguish their anarchism from that of Wolff, which must be called *moral* anarchism. *Political* anarchism is the doctrine which demands the dismantling of government, based on the assumption that the human community will be of a more morally worthy nature without governments than with them. We have already referred above to some writings of the anarchists to corroborate our claim that this expresses the nature of their attack on government and political order.

Moral anarchism, on the other hand, is the doctrine that one must be the determiner of one's own moral duties. It is the denial that the state—or for that matter any person or institution—has the right to create moral duties for an individual by fiat. This is Wolff's anarchism, and though I do not believe that it should be called anarchism, because of possible confusion with the

3. Leonard I. Krimerman and Lewis Perry, eds., *Patterns of Anarchy: A Collection of Writings in the Anarchist Tradition* (New York: Doubleday, 1966), pp. 11–12. Cf. also Horowitz, *The Anarchists,* pp. 186–7.

anarchist tradition of Proudhon and Bakunin, I generally agree with its conclusion. That is, I agree that an individual must be the determiner of his moral duty, because *moral* authority is a *contradictio in adjecto*.

But it should be abundantly clear that *moral* anarchism is a much different doctrine than *political* anarchism. This is evident from the fact that one can be a *moral* anarchist and deny the truth of *political* anarchism and vice versa. All that *moral* anarchism provides is that one should make one's own moral decisions even when confronted with the law of the state. *Political* anarchism starts from an *already-made moral decision* to the effect that governments and political systems are less moral in their effect than is their absence. A *moral* anarchist might consistently *not* reach this moral decision. He might find the presence of systems of official coercion generally more beneficial than their absence, while at the same time not acknowledging a moral "duty to obey the laws of the state *simply because they are the laws.*"[4]

On the other hand, one might live as a *political* anarchist in a human community with no system of official coercion and still forfeit one's moral autonomy. That is, it would be quite consistent with *political* anarchism—if unlikely—that a member of the community regarded the words of another as defining his moral duty, even though no form of coercion attached to those words.

The obligation suggested by moral autonomy can be spelled out in the proposition: One should be the determiner of one's own moral duties. This may lead to *moral* anarchism expressed in the proposition: One should reject the claim of any state to determine one's own moral duties. *But* this proposition in no way entails the proposition which is the core of *political* anarchism: The state should not exist. It should be abundantly clear that it is

4. Wolff, *Defense of Anarchism,* p. 18.

possible to hold the first proposition and deny the second, to be a *moral* anarchist and not a *political* anarchist.

Hence one can conclude that although a writer is free to define his terms as he will, there are some good reasons for avoiding linguistic anarchy, and Wolff has ignored those reasons in calling his doctrine "anarchism." *Moral* anarchism bears only the most superficial and largely misleading resemblance to *political* anarchism. Indeed what is truly mysterious about Wolff's essay is how very little is really being said and how awfully momentous it seems. I would suggest this has its source in the linguistic impropriety of using the term anarchism for a doctrine quite different from that which has borne this name in political philosophy. Wolff's essay gives the impression that what is being established is an a priori vindication of the anarchist tradition of Proudhon and Bakunin, when indeed all that is said is that a moral man should do what he thinks is moral—a notion which is hardly a defense of anarchism. Strictly speaking, Wolff's moral anarchism is compatible with any political system, since all that is necessary to be a *moral* anarchist is to deny that there is a moral duty to obey the law simply because it is the law. By Wolff's definition, the Nuremberg Tribunal, affirming a duty to disobey an immoral law or command, was promulgating anarchism.

IV. Is There a Moral Duty to Obey the Law?

> *Now let us recognize that every individual has a right to disagree with decisions of a court. But after those decisions are handed down, it is our obligation to obey the law whether we like it or not.*
>
> Richard M. Nixon
> New York Times

> *The same modern civilization which has given us unjust laws has given us great ideals. We need to learn how to violate these laws in such a way as to realize those ideals.*
>
> Howard Zinn
> *"The Conspiracy of Law"*

I have argued that a legitimate legal obligation is distinct from a moral obligation, *and* that a legitimate legal obligation has a moral force which is lacking from a command merely backed up by a threat of force. I have further argued that since the moral tests of a system of political authority and of individual moral duty largely overlap, it can be expected that legal obligations issuing from a legitimate state will largely overlap with the individual's moral obligation. This is one explanation of the fact that in general a legitimate state is regarded as one whose commands are morally binding.

It may strike the reader as strange to see this statement after a lengthy argument to the effect that legitimacy does not imply moral authority. But let us not fall into the trap which ensnared Wolff. While it is undoubtedly the case that legitimate states are generally regarded as states whose commands are morally binding on their citizens, this does not imply that this is the essence of legitimacy. This also does not imply that the commands of a legitimate state are ever absolutely morally binding, overriding the individual's conscientious decisions.

All that is implied here is what is implied in the overlap between the moral test of legitimacy and the moral test of the individual's personal moral duty. Since both are tested by their moral consequences, it is to be expected:

A. insofar as both judge accurately, there will be a good deal of overlap between the commands which a morally autonomous individual will give himself and those he will receive from a legitimate state; and

B. some of the moral reasons making a legitimate state legitimate will imply moral reasons for obeying its laws.

Proposition A should already be clear from our analysis of the moral justification of exercises of political authority. In this chapter, I will discuss proposition B. This should serve to clarify the proper relationship between political legitimacy and individual morality, and between legal obligation and moral obligation. It should also dispel any suggestion that it is the thrust of my argument to fly in the face of the conventional usage which does register some connection between political legitimacy and moral obligation.

Wolff, however, has inflated this "connection" into a definition: The commands of legitimate political authority constitute the moral duty of its subjects. The results of my analysis suggest that we are closer both to the technical and the ordinary usage of the term "legitimacy," if we characterize this "connection" as a correlation, which need not be perfect. The commands of legitimate political authority should correlate with correct judgments of individual moral duty, because both stem from one source: moral evaluation of the results of human actions. The correlation need not be perfect because of the different levels of generality and specificity at which this evaluation is carried out in the two cases; but the correlation should be positive and relatively high, because correct judgments at the general level cannot long differ from correct judgments at the specific level, and remain correct. So much for proposition A.

Looking beyond this to proposition B, we can raise the question as to whether there is a moral duty to obey the law, once it has been established as legitimate—*not* as a logical component of that legitimacy. By a moral duty we mean *a* moral duty, not the supreme and supervening moral duty. We certainly do not mean a moral duty to obey the law *simply because it is the law and regardless of other moral considerations or conflicting moral duties*. This is the type of duty to obey authority which Wolff assumes is implied in *political* authority, but which we have distinguished as *moral* authority and have argued is unthinkable.

Our question then reduces to the following: are there moral reasons for obeying the law of a legitimate political system that are indifferent to the content of any particular law? I believe the answer to this question is yes—but this clearly does not constitute a "duty to obey the laws of the state *simply because they are the laws*." So too, it in no way makes a claim that the law or the legal system entails a moral duty to be obeyed that overrides the individual's autonomous determination of his own duty. It points rather to a *prima facie* duty like that of keeping promises:

a duty which is obligatory in the absence of more compelling moral reasons.[1]

Rather, it suggests that when the individual is making his autonomous decision as to whether or not his moral duty lies in obeying or in resisting the law, there are *some* moral reasons for obeying the law just because it is the law of a legitimate state, and the morally autonomous individual ought to consider them in determining where his moral duty lies. In truth, our search for moral reasons for obeying the law could be equivalently expressed as the question: how does the fact that the law is legitimate enter into the deliberations of a moral individual deciding whether or not to obey the law?

Basically, these moral reasons derive from the notion that a legitimate political or legal system is a system which by definition generally tends toward the most morally worthy results possible given the facts of human nature and the level of human knowledge. This places on one an obligation not to act in such a way that may weaken or destroy this system or make it less productive of morally worthy results, and thus less legitimate. Insofar as (and of course this is not always the case) disobedience to the law tends to weaken or destroy the political or legal order, there are moral reasons for obeying the law because it is the law. Insofar as legitimacy is relative to moral results and therefore states can be more or less legitimate, the more legitimate is the state, the greater the moral duty not to act so as to undermine the political or legal order.[2]

From this consideration comes yet another moral reason for obeying the law of a legitimate state. Insofar as no individual can

1. Wolff, *Defense of Anarchism*, p. 18. Cf. John Searle, "How to Derive 'Ought' from 'Is,'" *Readings in Contemporary Ethical Theory*, ed. K. Pahel and M. Schiller (New Jersey: Prentice-Hall, 1970), pp. 157–8; also Hart, "Legal and Moral Obligation," p. 102.

2. On the possibility of degrees of legitimacy, cf. Fuller, *Morality of Law*, pp. 122, 147.

Kant ?

undermine or sustain the political system alone, each person's refraining from acting so as to undermine the legitimate system is based upon the expectation that others will also refrain. Insofar as one generally benefits from the fact that others refrain from undermining the system on the expectation that one will also refrain, there is a moral reason for obeying the law that is a species of the duty of reciprocity and which has led some to see the obligation to obey the law as resting upon a "contract."[3]

It should be clear that none of these moral reasons is conclusive, none establishes an overriding duty to obey the law regardless of other moral considerations. In some instances, for example—the civil disobedience that sparked the Civil Rights Acts of the last decade—the argument can be made that breaking the law tends more toward sustaining the legitimate political system or making it more legitimate than obeying the law. This is probably more likely to be the case when one is attacking the legitimacy of the particular law as inconsistent with the legal system, while not questioning the legitimacy of the legal system itself. One generally demonstrates this distinction in civil disobedience by accepting the legal punishment for the violation and thereby exhibiting one's acceptance of the legitimacy of the political system. Herein lies the difference between civil disobedience and revolution.

The moral reasons suggested above in no way constitute a duty to obey commands of legitimate authority regardless of one's autonomous moral decision. Rather, they sketch out some of the dimensions of the moral problem which confront the morally autonomous individual when he attempts to determine where his moral duty lies with regard to the law.

3. Cf. John Rawls, "Justice as Fairness," *The Philosophical Review,* 47 (April 1958): pp. 179ff; also Fuller, *Morality of Law,* pp. 19ff; and Hart, "Legal and Moral Obligation," p. 105; and Lon L. Fuller, "Human Interaction and the Law," in *The Rule of Law,* Robert Paul Wolff, ed. (New York: Simon and Schuster, 1971), pp. 171–217.

These are precisely the dimensions of the moral problem that confront Socrates as he awaits death in his prison cell. Socrates is a morally autonomous individual. He is in Wolff's terms an anarchist, because he accepts no higher determination of what he should do than what his reason dictates is the just course of action. He tells Crito, who has just suggested that he escape:

> We must reflect, then, whether we are to do as you say or not: for I am still what I always have been—a man who will accept no argument but that which on reflection I find to be truest.[4] We have to consider whether it is just or not for me to try to escape from prison, without the consent of the Athenians. If we find that it is just, we will try; if not, we will give up the idea.[5]

But when Socrates begins to determine which course of action is his duty, he has the laws step forth imaginarily and ask:

> Tell us, Socrates, what have you in mind to do? What do you mean by trying to escape but to destroy us, the laws and the whole state, so far as you are able? Do you think that a state can exist and not be overthrown, in which the decisions of law are of no force, and are disregarded and undermined by private individuals?[6]

It is interesting that this argument is telling for Socrates, since in the *Apology* he has given deliberate expression to his actual disobedience of the rulings of previous Athenian governments and of his intention to disobey the present Athenian government should it seek to deter him from engaging in philosophy. Socrates is no defender of unquestioning obedience of the state, and yet he accepts the state's verdict in the case of his own execution, persuaded largely by the argument just cited. How can we under-

4. Plato, *Crito,* in *Euthyphro, Apology, Crito,* trans. by F. J. Church and Robert D. Cumming (New York: The Library of Liberal Arts, 1956), p. 55.
5. Ibid., p. 57.
6. Ibid., p. 60.

stand this? It is certainly of little help to suggest, as Zinn does in *Disobedience and Democracy,* that "Socrates violates in the *Crito* the spirit he showed in the *Apology,* at his trial," or that Socrates is a "statist."[7] I think we can render the *Apology* and the *Crito* consistent by suggesting that Socrates believed that he should do no unjust thing, even if commanded by the state. On the other hand, he believed that under a good system of laws, the legal system has the moral right to issue commands and enforce them. For Socrates, to escape would be to suggest that this was a matter of power and not of right. Socrates acts so as to acknowledge the moral force of legal obligation without ever giving up acting upon his own determination of what his moral obligation is. His own solution to this problem is never to act contrary to his determination of his moral obligation, even if commanded to do so by the state. But at the same time never to act so as to undermine—if even only symbolically—the moral right of the legitimate state to enforce its commands.

Plato presents us in the *Crito* with that conflicting mesh of moral considerations which a morally autonomous man—indeed a *moral* anarchist—must take into account in determining his duty before the law. Significantly these include both a promise to obey the law which is implicit in Socrates living under and benefiting from the Athenian legal system, and an anticipation of the effects of disobedience upon that legal system which Socrates has acknowledged as legitimate.

---

7. Cf. Howard Zinn, *Disobedience and Democracy* (New York: Random House, 1968), p. 28.

V. Classical Democratic Theory and the Problem of Legitimacy

Political theories differ . . . over whether the state is a natural human institution serving inherent human needs or an artificial device brought into being to deal with problems of pre-political society . . . [T]he State may be described as an artificial contrivance brought into being for specific and limited purposes, which are however moral in character—this is the doctrine of John Locke and the generality of social contract theorists.

Robert Paul Wolff
Political Man and Social Man

. . . to secure these rights, Governments are instituted among Men, deriving their just powers from the consent of the governed. That whenever any Form of Government becomes destructive of these ends, it is the Right of the People to alter or to abolish it, and to institute new Government. . . .

Declaration of Independence, *1776*

After making the case against the possibility of a legitimate state in his first chapter, Wolff sets out in his second chapter to test the capacity of classical democratic theory to meet the challenge he has raised. That is, Wolff poses to classical democratic theory the problem which he has concluded is insoluble: that of reconciling the moral obligation to obey the law of the state with the duty of moral autonomy; *or equivalently:* that of demonstrating the principles upon which the legitimacy of the state could be based.

The largest segment of Wolff's essay is devoted to showing that, outside of the limiting case of unanimous direct democracy, classical democratic theory cannot solve the problem. On this basis, it might be suggested that I have devoted an inordinate amount of discussion to analysis of the foundation of Wolff's argument in his Chapter One, and not enough to the structure erected upon this foundation in his Chapter Two. The reply to this must be as follows: In arguing that Wolff has missed the uniquely *political* nature of political authority and with it the nature of the legitimacy of political systems, it must be concluded that Wolff's analysis of classical democratic theory falters, not because it emerges with wrong answers, *but because Wolff has posed the wrong problem.*

Defining legitimacy as the morally binding quality of the laws or the commands of the state and asking that classical democratic theory ground political legitimacy so defined, Wolff has posed a problem which is indeed insoluble for any political theory *but which no political theory has any need of solving.* With the foundation of his argument unearthed, the structure erected upon it must come tumbling down.

It remains simply to suggest in broad outline how classical democratic theory might respond to the proper problem of legitimacy. Let it be quite clear that Wolff's conclusion that classical democratic theory cannot supply us with principles establishing the commands of the state as *ipso facto* absolutely morally binding on the citizen is certainly correct. This would be tantamount to asking classical democratic theory to supply a justification for *moral* authority, and this we have seen, is a thoroughly meaningless notion. Hence, for the same reasons that Wolff's conclusion on this matter is correct, the problem which he poses for classical democratic theory is a meaningless problem.

On the other hand, classical democratic theory can be subjected to the test of political legitimacy, once this is recognized for what it is. The problem which must be posed is that of whether a political system based upon the principles which emerge from classical democratic theory will tend to yield more morally worthy results than can be expected from the absence of a political system, or, more morally worthy results than—or at least as much as—can be expected from other possible and viable political systems based on other political theories. Answering this question completely would take us far beyond the bounds of the present undertaking. All that I will attempt at this point is to sketch out in a bit more detail what this question would look like, in the hope of convincing the reader that the question *is* meaningful, and that it is *the* question of political legitimacy.

Since classical democratic theory operates at two distinct levels, the question must be raised at two levels. That is, classical democratic theory includes both theories of institutional design, e.g., majoritarianism, and theories of the justification for the institutions themselves, e.g., the social contract theory. The social contract theory is offered as a theory justifying the existence of democratic political institutions, and majoritarianism, as a device to best make those institutions work once they are accepted as justified.

First I will discuss the capacity of the social contract theory to provide principles of legitimate authority. Then I will indicate the key factors involved in assessing the legitimacy of majoritarian democracy.

A. Legitimacy and the Social Contract Theory*

The social contract theory is in general, as Michael Oakeshott says of Hobbes's *Leviathan* in particular:

> a myth, the transposition of an abstract argument into the world of the imagination. In it we are made aware at a glance of the fixed and simple center of a universe of complex and changing relationships.[1]

It is a representation in myth of the formation of human society out of presocial individuals, in just the same form as a scientist might imagine the combining of isolated atoms into a molecule. Like the mental experiment of the scientist, the aim of the social contract theory is not to reenact actual history, but rather to discover the principles upon which the combination is based. The social contract theory does not stand or fall on the historical issue of whether or not any state was ever so formed.

The social contract theory is a logical doctrine. It attempts, through a mental experiment, to break society into its presocial elements and determine the logic of social combination by imaginatively reconstructing the principles according to which the elements combine into a society. The social contract theory tries to resolve the paradox most poignantly phrased by Rousseau, "Men are free, and yet everywhere they are in chains." It tries to pass *logically,* via mental experiment, from the fact of human freedom to the fact of social constraint.

---

* This section was written prior to the appearance of John Rawls's *A Theory of Justice.* I think it is not premature to say that Rawls has taken a giant step toward accomplishing what I have merely tried to prove is possible: the development of principles of legitimate political authority based on the social contract theory.

1. Michael Oakeshott, "Introduction," to Thomas Hobbes, *Leviathan* (Oxford: Blackwell, 1960), p. xviii.

It makes the passage by imagining men, by definition totally free from social constraint, in the "state of nature." Such men quickly find that the total freedom of the "state of nature" makes them continual slaves—slaves to their fear of one another and to the need to continually protect themselves, actually or in anticipation. In other words, the total freedom of the state of nature is really a liability when it comes to the concrete freedoms which men seem to cherish: the freedom to enjoy the bounty of nature and community without fear, the freedom to set goals, to work, to accomplish one's goals and rest in the satisfaction thereof. Without even going so far as to suggest that the life of such "totally free" men would be solitary, poor, nasty, brutish and short, one can readily see how such men could hit upon a solution to their problem: Let's agree to give up some of our total freedom to gain the concrete freedoms we cherish, and let's establish the institutions to execute our agreement.

Here is a justification for social constraints infinitely more tractable to reasonable evaluation than the established justifications against which it was urged: the divine right of kings or the sinfulness of men in the fallen state. Where these justifications offered no standard by which the rationality of social controls could be tested, the social contract filled the gap. It suggested that all social controls be tested as to whether they indeed were necessary to ensure the concrete freedoms men really cherish. Any social control which does not meet this test, any social control which is merely the expression of the religious or emotional repugnance of one segment of the society to the acts of other segments must be judged irrational, *because it fails to satisfy the rationale for which free men take upon themselves social constraints*.

In brief, the social contract theory generates the following principles upon which a political system is to be based:

1. *The principle of the natural condition of man:* That the values and satisfactions of social life are possible only with some coercive system of social control (i.e., political authority).[2]

2. *The principle of natural right:* That men are free *by nature;* they are not given their freedom by society. Therefore, there is a *prima facie* case for freedom and against any limitation on freedom. The burden of proof for the introduction of a social control lies on him who would limit freedom, not on him who would maintain his freedom.

3. *The principle of the rational testability of social controls:* That the terms of this "burden of proof" are comparatively operationalizable: one must prove that a considered social control is one that rational men would freely take upon themselves, because it can be expected to lead to a net gain in the concrete freedoms men cherish.

4. *The principle of government by consent of the governed:* That since men are free by nature, they are the only source of any authority over them. Hence they are the ultimate court which must judge on the proof offered that a given social control is really rational and necessary.[3]

Without trying to defend these principles, granting indeed that with good reason an anarchist might reject the first, a Marxist the second, a Freudian the third, and a Platonist the fourth, we can still use these principles to suggest the proper approach to the issue of legitimacy.

Essentially, to deal with this problem one would have to imagine political systems based on these principles and compare them to systems based on other principles, and, of course, to the absence of any system. By "comparing" is meant anticipating the actual workings of systems or lack of system and the moral

2. Cf. ibid., p. lvi.
3. Cf. ibid., pp. lvii, lx.

value of the consequences likely to be produced. The emphasis must be placed on the "actual workings." In other words, it is not enough to say that granting unlimited power to a truly wise and good philosopher-king or psychoanalyst-king would be more likely to achieve moral ends than government by the people. This may indeed be so; but it is somewhat irrelevant. The issue is to imagine an actual system based on these principles. A system in which some men would actually have to test and select another man as "truly wise and good" and grant him total power.[4]

Such considerations have led men (perhaps even Wolff) to concur with Winston Churchill that democracy is the worst form of government except for all the others. What this means is that compared to the argument that some men are better equipped to rule than others, the arguments for democracy come up worst. But compared to the dangers implicit in actually selecting out some men to rule and the rest to be ruled, the actual practice of democracy comes up "least worst." This is especially so when we realize that the selection of some men to rule will be done by other men (and who will select them, or will they simply find themselves with the power to make the selection?); the selected rulers will not fall like manna from the principles of political philosophy.

The real test of the legitimacy of political systems based on the social contract theory would take the following form. Against anarchists, the truth of *the principle of the natural condition of man* would have to be defended. Against advocates of contending political philosophies, one would have to compare the anticipated actual workings of systems recognizing some rights as natural, with ones which regard all rights as socially or legally

---

4. Cf. John Rawls, "Two Concepts of Rules," *Theories of Ethics*, Philippa Foot, ed. (New York: Oxford University Press, 1971), pp. 150–153.

created. One would have to compare the anticipated actual workings of systems regarding all social controls as rationally testable with systems claiming divine right or mystical inspiration from the *Volk* for their decrees. One would have to compare the anticipated actual workings of systems locating final political authority in the consent of the governed with ones which consult only the governors, or perhaps only some of the governed.

Upon the basis of these comparisons, a judgment that political systems based on the principles which emerge from the social contract theory would tend to yield more morally worthy results than can be expected from the absence of a political system, or more morally worthy results than—or at least as much as—can be expected from other possible and viable political systems issuing from other political theories, *is equivalent to the judgment that the social contract theory is a theory of the principles of the legitimate state.* That is, it corresponds precisely to Wolff's definition of what a political philosophy ought to do.[5]

None of this is altered by the fact that such judgments about legitimacy are by no means easy to establish and may indeed never hope to go beyond the truth status of scientific theories. This is precisely why there is still life in political philosophy. Nor is this altered by the fact that states professing to be democracies may not live up to the principles of classical democratic theory. Indeed it is only by presupposing the possibility of such judgments as to the legitimacy of political systems that one could ever criticize a particular political system as illegitimate. It is worthy of note that Wolff's analysis leaves us with no standard to judge the legitimacy of particular political systems. He writes:

> A man might find that his affairs flourished in a dictatorship or monarchy, and even that the welfare of the people as a whole was effectively advanced by the policies of such a state. Democracy, then, could claim to be no more than one type of *de*

5. Wolff, *In Defense of Anarchism,* pp. 3–5, *inter alia.*

facto government among many, and its virtues, if any, would be relative. Perhaps, as Winston Churchill once remarked, democracy is the worst form of government except for all the others; but if so, then the "citizens" of America are as much subjects of an alien power as the Spaniards under Franco or the Russians under Stalin. They are merely more fortunate in their rulers.[6]

B. Legitimacy and Majority Rule

I am skipping over Wolff's arguments about representative democracy, since these are arguments against the feasibility of representation, not against the principle of representative democracy. These arguments can be summed up by saying that I have no "obligation to obey laws which are made in my name by a man who has no obligation to vote as I would."[7] In truth this refers to a "representative" with no obligation to "represent" me. Presumably, if he really would represent me, I would be morally bound. Or so Wolff implies in the following two statements:

> So long as I do not, either in person or through my agent, join in the enactment of the laws by which I am governed, I cannot justly claim to be autonomous.[8]

> If a citizen cannot even find a *candidate* whose views coincide with his own, then there is no possibility at all that he will send to the parliament a genuine *representative*[9] (emphasis in the original).

Wolff's argument here is not that representative democracy is illegitimate in principle. Really his argument hinges on how unlikely it is that one will be truly represented by one's "repre-

6. Ibid., p. 40.
7. Ibid., p. 29.
8. Ibid., p. 30.
9. Ibid., p. 33.

sentatives." Nothing is implied about the legitimacy of representative democracy, should it work. The implication of the passages cited above is that representation might be acceptable, were one truly represented.

On the other hand, majority rule is attacked by Wolff as illegitimate in principle, with the definition of legitimacy which Wolff has used from the beginning:

> we must inquire whether the members of a democratic polity are morally bound to obey the decisions of the majority, and if so, why.[10]

And, as if this weren't impossible enough, Wolff stipulates that this magical morally binding quality must derive from the nature of "majority rule" itself.

> If we hold that majority rule has some special validity, then it must be because of the character of majority rule itself.[11]

By now it should be clear that the search for a morally binding quality emerging from a decision-making procedure is a search for a nonexistent needle in a haystack. By stipulating that this morally binding quality be found in the nature of "majority rule" itself, Wolff has now asked us to search for a nonexistent needle in an *invisible* haystack.

Even Wolff has recognized that majoritarianism is a *device* to overcome the obstacles to unanimous direct democracy, which for Wolff is legitimate.[12] Hence the question of the moral status or legitimacy of majority rule must be cognizant of its instrumental nature. It is a tool designed to achieve an end. It must be judged as to its effectiveness in achieving that end, and its moral

10. Ibid., p. 38.
11. Ibid., pp. 42–43.
12. Ibid., p. 27.

value must be regarded as derivative, i.e., as having its source in the moral value of that end.

There can be no legitimacy—by Wolff's definition or mine—found intrinsic to majority rule. The moral value of majority rule derives from the moral value of the democratic theory upon which it is based. If there is legitimacy to a system of majority rule, it stems from the legitimacy of *the principle of government by consent of the governed.* Majority rule must be judged, in comparison to other such devices for achieving decisions, as to its ability to translate the "consent of the governed" into the "commands of government" when the governed disagree.

To this Wolff would no doubt reply that by this standard "*any* method of decision-making . . . would be equally legitimate."[13] The answer to this is, Yes, but. . . . And the "but" is quite significant.

Since no intrinsic legitimacy is claimed for majority rule, it might appear that it is merely one device for achieving decision among many, such as unanimous consensus, drawing of lots or consulting of oracles, with no particular claim to legitimacy. *But* there is one unique fact about majority rule which distinguishes it from all other devices for reaching a decision when the citizens are in disagreement. Theoretically, of course, no device for translating the consent of the governed into the acts of government is superior to unanimity. However, in practice, since decisions are always between alternative courses of action and since people do disagree, unanimity can mean that one hold-out decides for all the rest. So too, consulting of oracles or drawing of lots, or requiring of two-thirds majority, for that matter, can all effectively mean that a minority has its way over a majority. The *only* decision-achieving device which rules this out in principle as a possibility is majority rule.

13. Ibid., p. 42.

This is, of course, no guarantee that majority rule will choose the most moral course of action. But since there is no such guarantee built into any decision-achieving device, and since decision must be achieved, majority rule recommends itself because of all devices possible, it alone precludes minority rule.

The unique claim to legitimacy which majority rule has, which comes to it from the legitimacy of *the principle of government by consent of the governed,* lies in the fact that it is the *only* system for translating the consent of the governed into the commands of government, which in principle rules out the possibility of a minority having its way over a majority. No other decision-achieving device can make this claim.

Of course, if one is still in quest of the chimera of moral authority, this *relative* and *derivative* legitimacy of majority rule will give little solace. If one accepts as the test of legitimacy the comparison of the anticipated effects of possible institutional arrangements, and if one compares the workings of majority rule—carried out according to principle—with any other system, one is likely to find that majority rule is the worst method of reaching a decision except for all others.

VI. Finding the Proper Path for Political Philosophy

Indeed, we may wonder whether the absence of all constraint is conducive to the development of individuality itself, or whether perhaps judicious social limitations upon individual action might not actually be a better way of nurturing a truly autonomous person.

Robert Paul Wolff
The Poverty of Liberalism

Concepts, first employed to make things intelligible, are clung to even when they make them unintelligible. Thus it comes that when once you have conceived things as "independent," you must proceed to deny the possibility of any connexion whatsoever among them, because the notion of connexion is not contained in the definition of independence.

William James
"The Compounding of Consciousness"

We must only divide where there is a real cleavage between specific forms.

Plato
The Statesman

A large portion of the writings of William James can be characterized as an eloquent warning against mistaking the world of concepts for the world, against forgetting that "Reality, life, experience, concreteness, immediacy, use what word you will, exceeds our logic, overflows and surrounds it."[1] James does not, of course, deny the importance of concepts:

> All these abstract concepts are but as flowers gathered, they are only moments dipped out from the stream of time, snapshots taken, as by a kinetoscopic camera, at a life that in its original coming is continuous. Useful as they are as samples of the garden, or to re-enter the stream with, or to insert in our revolving lantern, they have no value but these practical values. . . . For you cannot make continuous being out of discontinuities, and your concepts are discontinuous.[2]

Wolff fails to heed James's warning.

The central thrust of the critique of Wolff's essay could be summed up by saying that Wolff defends a type of anarchism from which no political program issues. For this reason we have characterized it as *moral* anarchism, to be distinguished from *political* anarchism. None of this prevents Wolff from trying to extract an anarchist political program from his argument in his final chapter. If my analysis is correct, then this passage to political anarchism in the last portion of Wolff's essay is not warranted by the arguments in the earlier portions of his essay. Making the illegitimate nature of this passage clear will serve both to yield additional evidence as to the political irrevelance of Wolff's anarchism and to suggest the dangers for political philosophy which lurks at the heart of Wolff's approach.

1. William James, "The Compounding of Consciousness," *The Writings of William James,* John J. McDermott, ed. (New York: The Modern Library, 1968), pp. 557–558.

2. William James, "Bergson and His Critique of Intellectualism," in *Writings of William James,* p. 565.

It is at once remarkable and to be expected that when Wolff comes to discuss *political* anarchism, he implicitly accepts the consequences of political institutions as the locus of the test of their moral validity—that is, he implicitly accepts the moral test of legitimacy which has been advocated in the present essay. He recognizes that the "truest test of the political philosophy of anarchism" is that of whether there is "any way in which these ends [the ends for which men actually congregate] could be served other than by commands enforced by coercion and by the myth of legitimacy."[3] What Wolff fails to see is that this test is in no way implied in the anarchism which he defends as "the only political doctrine consistent with the virtue of autonomy."[4]

Indeed, Wolff's anarchism is consistent with *any* political system, with *any* political program—so long as one reserves for himself the "final decisions about what one should do."[5] So long as he does not regard the master's commands as morally binding upon him, the slave in chains is as much a Wolffian anarchist as the most committed follower of Proudhon. So long as the committed Nazi does not regard the Fuehrer's commands as morally binding in themselves, so long as he merely complies because the Fuehrer's commands coincide with the results of his own moral deliberations, he satisfies the requirements which Wolff establishes for anarchism at the opening of his discussion.

That a Wolffian *moral* anarchist may adopt *political* anarchism as a political program may be a psychological likelihood, *but it is in no way necessitated by his acceptance of moral anarchism.* When Wolff slips unannounced from *moral* anarchism to *political* anarchism in his final chapter, this is precisely a result of not heeding the Jamesian warning: it is a result of mistaking the

3. Wolff, *Defense of Anarchism,* pp. 79–80.
4. Ibid., p. 18.
5. Ibid., p. 15.

abstract concepts which he has used to cut up the real world for the realities of that world.

Fundamentally this is a failure on Wolff's part to see that the *moral* autonomy which he defends is barely the palest image of the concrete *political* autonomy for which men struggle and die. Wolff's *moral* autonomy is the purely inner freedom of the Cartesian ego, to say *no* to all claims to legitimacy. It presupposes no real dependence upon the world for the *power* to say—and to live—that *no*. It is by failing to see that real human *moral* autonomy, as opposed to the concept of *moral* autonomy, depends on *political* autonomy because it depends on *power*—the power to think, the ability to inquire and investigate, perhaps even to experiment—which in turn depends on the support and cooperation of the social order, that Wolff gives us an anarchism without a political program. After all, *political* is little more than the adjectival form of *power*.

As soon as the relationships of autonomy to power and of power to society are granted, then the conceptual antithesis of autonomy and authority is revealed as a mere abstraction. It is an example of precisely what the Eleatic Stranger has warned against, a division where no real cleavage exists. Power is the subterranean tunnel which links autonomy and authority.

Legitimate political authority is the legitimate use of force to create or maintain a social order. If real *moral* autonomy is a moral value, and if it is dependent on *political* autonomy, and if *political* autonomy is dependent on a social order—as Wolff himself recognizes in *The Poverty of Liberalism*[6]—then there can be some forms of *political authority legitimated by moral autonomy itself*. But this can only be seen once one departs from the rarified heights of the concepts of autonomy and authority and begins to explore the real conditions of *moral* autonomy. Conceptually, *moral* autonomy depends on nothing but

6. Wolff, *Poverty of Liberalism*, pp. 26–27.

the metaphysical postulates of human freedom and rationality. In reality, *moral* autonomy depends on *political* autonomy. It depends on the availability of power—to think, to inquire, to evaluate, to experiment, to accumulate and exchange and test ideas—and this depends on the social order. This is why a conceptual analysis of autonomy and authority—such as Wolff presents—can never yield a political philosophy, though it may deceive us into thinking that it has, through the manipulation of politically tinged notions. It is, however, a purely formal analysis, devoid of politically fateful content.

Only analysis of the real conditions of human autonomy, indeed of human *moral* autonomy, can yield a *political philosophy*. "There is," as Dewey writes, "an intrinsic connection between choice as freedom and power of action as freedom." That is, between *moral* autonomy and *political* autonomy.

> A choice which intelligently manifests individuality enlarges the range of action, and this enlargement in turn confers upon our desires greater insight and foresight, and makes choice more intelligent. There is a circle, but an enlarging circle, or, if you please, a widening spiral.[7]

And therefore,

> The question of political and economic freedom is not an addendum or afterthought, much less a deviation or excrescence, in the problem of personal freedom. For the conditions that form political and economic liberty are required in order to realize the potentiality of freedom each of us carries with him in his very structure.[8]

Interestingly enough, one could cite passages in abundance from Wolff's third chapter to demonstrate Wolff's awareness of

7. John Dewey, *Philosophy and Civilization* (New York: Minton, Balch and Company, 1931), p. 286.
8. Ibid., p. 268.

precisely this dependence of autonomy on social conditions. He writes:

> There would appear to be no alternative but to embrace the doctrine of anarchism and categorically deny *any* claim to legitimate authority by one man over another. Yet I confess myself unhappy with the conclusion that I must simply leave off the search for legitimate collective authority. Perhaps it might be worth saying something about the deeper philosophical reasons for this reluctance.
>
> Man confronts a natural world which is irreducibly *other,* which stands over against him, independent of his will and indifferent to his desires. . . . Man also confronts a social world which *appears* other, which *appears* to stand over against him, at least partially independent of his will and frequently capricious in its frustration of his desires. Is it folly to suppose that this opposition can be overcome, and that man can so perfectly conquer society as to make it his tool rather than his master?[9] (emphasis in the original).

Here Wolff is groping toward the social conditions of autonomy, and his answer to the question is guardedly optimistic.

> To be sure, insofar as men are ignorant of the total structures of the institutions within which they play their several roles, they will be victims of consequences unintended by anyone; and, of course, to the extent that men are set against one another by conflicting interests, those whose institutional roles give them advantages of power or knowledge in the social struggle will prevail over those who are relatively disadvantaged. But *since each man's unfreedom is entirely a result either of ignorance or of a conflict of interests,* it ought to be in principle possible for a society of rational men of good will to eliminate the domination of society and subdue it to their wills in a manner that is impossible in the case of nature[10] (emphasis added).

9. Wolff, *In Defense of Anarchism,* p. 72.
10. Ibid., p. 76.

Here the relationship of freedom or unfreedom to power and the social order, to the ability to think and evaluate and to the support and cooperation of fellow men, is made quite explicit. But this freedom is something far different from *moral* autonomy. This is clear as soon as we recognize that, though Wolff suggests that *unfreedom* may result from ignorance or conflict of interests, *forfeiture of moral autonomy does not!* In the condition of unfreedom which results from ignorance or conflict of interests, one may retain one's moral autonomy, so long as one "does not neglect the duty of attempting to ascertain what is right,"[11] so long as one makes "the final decisions about what one should do."[12]

Thus when Wolff refers to autonomy in the following passage, we have no choice but to suspect that the autonomy to which he now refers is not the *moral* autonomy upon which he has based his earlier argument for anarchism. He writes:

> It should now be clear why I am unwilling to accept as final the negative results of our search for a political order which harmonizes authority and autonomy. The state is a social institution. . . . When rational men, in full knowledge of the proximate and distant consequences of their actions, determine to set private interest aside and pursue the general good,

in brief, when the conditions necessitating political systems no longer exist,

> it *must* be possible for them to create a form of association which accomplishes that end without depriving some of them of their moral autonomy. The state, in contrast to nature, cannot be ineradicably *other*[13] (emphasis in the original).

If a morally autonomous man could live in a dictatorship, as Wolff suggests on more than one occasion, how is it possible that

11. Ibid., p. 13.
12. Ibid., p. 15.
13. Ibid., p. 78.

any form of political association could deprive some men of their moral autonomy? The moral autonomy upon which Wolff constructs his defense of anarchism is a purely inner fact, possible for any person metaphysically free and rational. Thus, short of being drugged or hypnotized or killed, no man can be deprived of his moral autonomy except by freely forfeiting it. The moral autonomy which a social organization can deprive a man of must be a type of autonomy which is dependent on social organization. But such an autonomy must—by that very fact of dependence—not be ineradicably opposed to authority. Indeed such an autonomy may justify, and can well depend for its existence upon, judicious exercise of authority.

Wolff has fallen directly into the trap against which James has warned. He has defined his concepts as independent and cannot get them into connection without altering their definitions. Autonomy, defined as determining for oneself what one ought to do, and authority, defined as having what one ought to do determined by another, are simply and absolutely irreconcilable. When Wolff faces this, he admits that "the arguments of [his] essay suggest that the just state must be consigned to the category of the round square, the married bachelor, and the unsensed sense-datum."[14] When he shrinks from facing this, he must slip from his early definition of moral autonomy to one which no longer a priori excludes legitimate authority, and therefore one which bears no resemblance to the duty of moral autonomy upon which Wolff's defense of anarchism is based.

But this slipping between definitions, though a danger ever present to the conceptual approach, is not necessary. It results from the fact that Wolff has not adequately analyzed the concept of political authority. As I have tried to demonstrate in the major portion of the present essay, there is no a priori op-

14. Ibid., p. 71.

position between the concept of moral autonomy and that of legitimate political authority, and thus that there is no a priori argument from the former concept to the political doctrine of anarchism.

Let us not be deceived, however. Such clarification of concepts may be a prerequisite for political philosophy, but it is not itself political philosophy, and it is extremely misleading to think that it is. The real work of political philosophy begins where we are leaving off. Its task lies in determining the real connections between the things human beings value—such as moral autonomy —and the forms of political association—the systems of political authority—which sustain or thwart those things. The challenge of anarchism, the claim that the things human beings value are best sustained without forms of political authority, is neither proven nor refuted in Wolff's essay nor in mine. All I have tried to do is to demonstrate that such a claim cannot be established from a conceptual analysis of autonomy and authority, and that political philosophy—the "discovery, analysis, and demonstration of the forms and principles of legitimate authority"[15] lives.

15. Ibid., p. 5.

Index

72 73 74 75   12 11 10 9 8 7 6 5 4 3 2 1